Lancashire Mill Town
Traditions

The Dalesman Publishing Company Ltd.
Clapham (via Lancaster), North Yorkshire

First published 1977

© W. R. Mitchell, 1977

ISBN: 0 85206 414 4

Printed by Galava Printing Company Ltd.
Hallam Road, Nelson, Lancashire

Lancashire Mill Town Traditions

by W. R. Mitchell

Dalesman Books

1977

CPSIA information can be obtained at www.ICGtesting.com
Printed in the USA
LVOW07s0032030715

444796LV00001B/59/P

Contents

The Illustrations

Colour Picture: from a painting by J. J. Thomlinson

Back Cover: Top left—Preparing a warp for the loom; right—a Lancashire weaver; Bottom—Early bus exersion from Burnley to York Minster.

Map of the Cotton Towns by E. Gower

CLITHEROE

COLNE

BARROWFORD

NELSON

BRIERFIELD

PADIHAM

BURNLEY

PRESTON

ACCRINGTON

BLACKBURN

DARWEN

TODMORDEN

CHORLEY

RAWTENSTALL

ROCHDALE

BOLTON

BURY

OLDHAM

MANCHESTER

STOCKPORT

An Introduction

Y EARS ago, I was standing on Stockport station when a steam-hauled passenger train appeared, breathing smoke and soot. A porter shouted, melodiously and with pride: "Manchester Victoria, Bolton, Accrington, Blackburn, Burnley, Nelson and Colne." His voice quickened as the names became shorter. The last word was hurled away just before the locomotive ran beside the platform, when the hiss of steam made further talk impossible.

The names, and the jaunty manner in which they were delivered, came to mind when I devised this book. It would be based mainly on the heartland of Lancashire, in and around the towns listed by the railway porter. I did not want to produce yet another history of the cotton industry, but to hear the voices of the older Lancashire folk talking about mill town life and culture in a period that is still fairly easily recalled: from 1900 to 1935. I would faithfully record what people told me about days that are historically recent but now have curiosity value. The brave new Lancashire is not dependent upon cotton mills. It is cleaner and tidier than it was. The people are more affluent and better nourished than were their parents and grandparents.

During the first 35 years of this century, the reign of King Cotton began a decline that continues to this day. Yet when the century opened he had about 400,000 slaves in the Lancashire valleys. Over 1,000 mills sustained the late Victorian and Edwardian trade expansion, generating much of the wealth that was poured into investment overseas. So immense was the Lancashire cotton industry at its peak that by breakfast-time on any working day the looms had met the demands of the home market. The rest of the cloth they produced could be exported.

By the end of the 19th century, about one-third of Lancashire was covered with mills, terraced houses, flagstones and cobbles.

Industrial areas had been hurriedly grafted on to historic towns. Villages became sprawling communities in which new factories and homes were tastelessly intermingled, bound together by soot. The inflow of labour from many parts of Britain had made the cotton region one of the most densely-populated areas in Europe.

What was it really like to work in the mills in grandmother's day, or even when mother was young? How did people cope with the often squalid conditions in back-to-back housing as flecks of soot descended from a forest of chimneys ? What were the customs, beliefs, pastimes and domestic routines of the people who sustained the world's first industrial revolution?

The minds of the veterans I met tended to filter out the grimmest memories, retaining those that were counted attractive, not least the rich community life of the towns and local patriotism engendered by mill, street and place of worship. I heard of the days when the knocker-up went on his unwelcome rounds, and of the quirks of small-time mill bosses and their overlookers —the tacklers—who were the butt of many jokes. I was told about the days of "poverty knock", of household tasks like baking and washing that demanded strength as well as brains, of schooldays and highpoints in religious life, such as the Whit Walks organised by the Sunday Schools. Many a work-seamed face lit up at the mention of Wakes Week and the annual exodus from mill town to Blackpool.

Stories and songs invest the old days with romance. They were not so romantic to live through. Look at the old photographs in library collections, of dour towns, work-weary people and thin-faced, be-capped street urchins, many of them with bare feet. Consider the massed machines in spinning mill and weaving shed, where the workers spent most of their conscious hours. Two-thirds of the operatives were children in fact or status, and shabby ranks of unemployed, providing a reservoir of cheap reserve labour, wandered from mill to mill in the early morning.

The lass who went clatteringly to work in clogs and shawl became the romantic "Sally", the pride of our alley, or the pert "Lassie from Lancashire". With such old songs, during the depressing 1930s, did Miss Gracie Fields from Rochdale raise our spirits. Gracie knew what she was singing about, for as a mill winder she rose at 5 a.m. and trudged for a mile, aiming to be at her workplace by 6 a.m. Her mother was a weaver who considered that Gracie had "a posher job", being able to leave work in a relatively clean state. Gracie's younger sister was employed, half-time, sweeping beneath the machines and returned home filthy!

I recall a film sequence, with Gracie and her Lancashire lasses moving arm-in-arm between massed mills and houses, with "Sing as We Go" on their lips. The personality and the songs are typical of the spinning area: Rochdale, Oldham, Bolton. Here the cotton itself seems to sing as it is processed. The weavers amid the clatter of the sheds in towns and villages further east had less to sing about.

There was a time when everyone in the mill towns could recite a line or two from Waugh and Leacock. They did so painstakingly, for it was in dialect. This form, popular with writers in the latter part of the 19th century, was carried on effectively and with good humour by T. Thompson. Stanley Houghton and Harold Brighouse dramatised the outlook of the forthright, clearheaded Lancashire lass in *Hindle Wakes* and *Hobson's Choice*, in which plays the roles of maister and weyver, rich and poor, became stylised. Walter Greenwood, in novels and plays, dwelt on the grim times of trade recession; and while expressing deeplyfelt sorrow over the circumstances of the downtrodden, his work, perversely, added to the romance.

The downtrodden could either laugh or cry. In most cases, they preferred to laugh. At about the time of the Great Depression, the early 1930s, it was reported that treacle mines existed at Sabden, and that weavers produced parkin on their looms, using oatmeal as warp and treacle as weft. By that time, the cinema offered a few hours of escape from life's grim realities. It provided romantic slush or moments of high comedy, such as the time when George Formby, complete with ukulele, was at his prime and caught the spirit of Wakes Week with his "A Little Stick of Blackpool Rock".

Up to the 1930s, the Marriott Edgar monologues, including "Albert and the Lion", were in vogue. Now the humour of Sandy Powell and Norman Evans brought a response, and Frank Randall, a Lancashire comedian, flashed his toothless grin from screen or stage. Millions of people derive impressions of Lancashire through the long-running television series *Coronation Street*—which, like the works of Walter Greenwood, was set in Salford and has a big city environment. One can recognise some distinctive Lancashire characteristics in the hair-netted, puritanical Ena Sharples, played by a Lancashire actress, Violet Carson, while Annie Walker, who presides over *The Rover's Return*, is the off-cummed-un who has become a native. In old-time urban Lancashire, The Street was an entity.

The artist Lowry came near to fixing the overwhelming impression of grim, unrelenting factory routine; of the masses who existed in the cheerless world of mills and houses set down on the grid-iron pattern, without regard to topography. Helen Bradley has been truer to life, blending the grim and gay in a succession of lively studies that have authentic Lancashire—its terraced streets and millscapes—in the background.

The real Lancashire is hard to define. No two cotton towns were alike. There was half a world of difference between, say, Bolton and Burnley. What the Lancashire towns had in common was their close proximity to the countryside. Sometimes, it was represented in the millscape as a sliver of green that was faintly perceived through a haze of smoke from factory, home and railway locomotive: three prime pollutants. The countryside could none the less be reached in half an hour's steady walking, and elements of the old rural nature of Lancashire endured as annual customs enacted in even the most deprived areas, where scarcely a blade of grass grew. Operatives in small village concerns lived in a semi-rural state in which they could keep faith with their countryside origins.

In the people of urban Lancashire one finds a fusion of cultures. In Burnley, for example, there has been a strong Irish flavour. Naturally, there was a basic realism, but this was always tempered by humanity. A cotton operative tended to laugh at himself or herself—or at life. Lancashire mill town humour was usually laconic, tongue-in-cheek, by no means as "cutting" as in Liverpool.

The cotton industry endures, but in a greatly reduced form. It has been in steady recession for at least 60 years, and during the last two decades nearly all the remaining private companies have gone, to be absorbed into the combines. The old Lancashire depended greatly on the first-hand relationship between employer and worker, as evidenced by his use of Christian names and the former's regular inquiries into the latter's family matters.

Sixty per cent of Lancashire's old market is now met by overseas competitors. Sixty per cent of the fabric used in Britain today is imported. Lancashire weaves on. It weaves fine fabrics —and wicks for oil lamps used as far away as Japan. The nose-cone of the world's most advanced aircraft, *Concorde*, was woven on a Lancashire loom that was 50 years old. Today, rather more than 50% of the textile operatives are of Asian origin.

Many people have helped me to muster the information used in this book. Special thanks are extended to: Rex Brindle, Harry Cox, Deacons of Belmont, Bob Dobson, Stanley Ellis, Madge Emmott, John Finch, Jimmy Fishwick, Green Bros., Sam Hanna, Mike Harding, Martin Hoole, Stanley Jeeves, Mary Kendall, Eric Lomax, Frank Lowe, Norman Mitchell, Roy Rowley, Olive Sharples. The ever-helpful staffs of the libraries at Burnley, Colne and Nelson allowed me to copy the photographs from their local collections.

Lancashire Cotton

LANCASHIRE'S rapid rise as the world's first industrial society began in the 18th century. The steam engine was developed, leading to the mechanisation of processes connected with textiles. A century later, the Lancashire cotton industry was large and complex.

Why did Lancashire attract such development to a greater degree than other western regions of Britain? One advantage mentioned for Lancashire is pure, soft water, flowing liberally from the gritstone moors of the Pennines and their outliers. Some other regions intercept the clouds that have swept across the Atlantic, and before long the rivers of the valleys were far from pure as industry used them as open sewers. The bleachers and dyers depended on water they dammed in pockets of the higher hills.

What Lancashire did have was cheap fuel—deposits of coal which soon were being mined in an area of about 500 square miles. Pits in the basin dominated by Burnley and Blackburn were especially productive, handy to the cotton mills and, via the Leeds and Liverpool canal, to towns lying to the east. By the late 1850s, Lancashire's mines were yielding some 10m. tons of coal a year.

There was, in Lancashire, scope for development. The land over which the new towns spread was relatively poor, its population quite small. Farmers who clung to their poor, cold little holdings grumbled at the heavy rainfall, though this was another blessing for the textile industry. To be successfully processed, cotton demanded humidity. More significantly, Lancashire had Liverpool—a developing port which had already established close trading links with America, through which came the first major shipments of cotton.

The Golden Years

The period of most rapid growth was the second half of the 19th century, during which a railway system had been developed to speed the transportation of goods. As the new century dawned, most of the terraced houses we see today were occupied and urban conditions, though generally poor, were improving.

Lancashire textiles reached a peak of productivity just before the 1914-18 war, and in the last great period of expansion the industrial potential was staggering. Bolton's spinning mills alone absorbed the total yield of cotton from the Nile Valley. Elm Street in Burnley had mills holding 10,000 looms. It was computed in 1914 that the mills of Oldham and district held as many spindles as did France and Germany combined. And what mills! The most modern soared to five or six storeys and had brick-built chimneys topping 150 feet. It was said of one firm that it built a chimney of such magnificence there was no money left to cover the cost of the mill!

New civic buildings emulated the largest of the mills in size and grandeur. Civic pride was developing. The rise to prominence in local government had not yet robbed the local tycoon of his ability to sway local affairs. In case future generations might forget their names, the factory owners enshrined them in the form of gifts. At Accrington, for example, William Peel presented 35 acres of land that became incorporated in the 93 acres of Peel Park. This was in 1909, when all was well with the world. Four years later, Thomas Bullough handed over the land that became Bullough Park. It provided a much-needed amenity in a town that was built as little more than a workplace and dormitory for the workers. The giants of industry occupied big houses at the most salubrious edges of the towns, or new villas standing at St. Annes or Southport. They had not yet had their ambitions thwarted by taxation.

By 1912, over 85 per cent of the cotton being produced in Lancashire was being exported. In that year, over 600,000 workers produced 8,000 million yards of cloth. Burnley had 100,000 looms and Nelson possessed 50,000. Already in the industry were the seeds of its destruction, for between 1900 and 1914 a total of £96m. of textile machinery was exported. Other nations began the process of industrialisation, based—as Lancashire's had been—on cotton; they were assisted by some of the most ingenious machinery that Lancashire brains could devise. For a time, the threat from overseas competitors was masked by the fact that Lancashire businessmen did not take it seriously. Nor need they —during the golden years.

War stopped the industry's heady progress. In 1914, trading abruptly terminated. In a matter of weeks many of the mills were closed. Thousands of operatives were without work.

Boom and Decline

In the boom trade following the ending of wartime restrictions, Lancashire again met the major demand for cotton. Its customer was the world. Some companies declared dividends of about 40 per cent. It was the last great fling.

The war had shattered the English social structure. Men returning from a conflict that did not appear to have been fought for any special reason were disillusioned, and in April, 1922 they were naturally bitter when wages were reduced by 40 per cent (they declined by a further 10 per cent in the following October). A weaver with four looms received about 22s. a week. Before the war, a man did not feel he could afford to have a union membership card; his loyalty to an anti-union boss was often derived from fear of dismissal. Now the unions gained ground.

On to Lancashire's special trading difficulties was added a world trade recession, following the Wall Street crash. It led to the worst depression in living memory. The effect on Lancashire's mill towns was not uniform. Bolton, for example, had flexibility, and when a spinning mill was lost the labour force might be absorbed in new concerns: small engineering projects and the like. Some towns, notably the weaving centres to the east, suffered the fate of allegiance to a single big industry: cotton. There were minor variations. Nelson, noted for its finer cloth, was less badly affected than nearby Burnley and Colne.

Unemployment at Blackburn soared in 1931 and in some smaller towns reached 60%. In the following years, the population declined. Between 1929 and 1939, the Blackburn Sub Region lost 17,538 people, or 13·9% of the insured population. Gandhi, visiting Lancashire in 1931, strummed his own personal spinning wheel as he listened to the lament by industrial leaders over India's unco-operative attitude with regard to tariffs. Gandhi was pre-occupied with the distress he knew existed in India.

By the mid-1930s, some renewal of confidence was detectable, and in 1937 the production of cotton cloth reached about half the 1912 level. Rayon was being introduced, heralding the age of man-made fibres. Between the wars, some 800 cotton mills were closed, partly as the result of government action. Whenever an election was due, the politicians would suddenly become sympathetic to the cotton trade, which was assisted in return for the closure of a specific number of mills.

A major reason for the decline of Lancashire cotton was the rising cost of labour. The impressive profits of the past had been accrued through having a large reservoir of cheap labour. Children joining the mills as half-timers were unpaid for several months. When trained, they might eventually reach the handsome wage of 5s. a week. If they were mule-spinners, they became "little piecers" and could do this work until they were anything up to 25 years of age. "Side piecers" might be even older. A man of 35 years of age could still be waiting for a man's job—enduring a pitiable wage in the hope of becoming a craftsman at £2 10s. up to £3, which was the situation in the late 1920s.

What defeated the Lancashire cotton industry as a major world factor was, in the end, the rise in the school-leaving age. The initiative was claimed by some eastern countries where child labour was, and is, a matter of daily economics.

The Mills

THE Lancashire textile industry has four main components: spinning and weaving (referred to as manufacturing), finishing and merchandising. A square yard of cloth contains about a mile of thread, and in the old days it took six floors holding spinning machinery to assuage the appetite of looms occupying an equivalent amount of space.

Spinning

Five storeys were common in the historical period; occasionally there would be six. In the heyday of spinning, when mills grew like mushrooms in places like Oldham and Rochdale, a manufacturer might order a complete mill: building and equipment. He would merely stipulate the desired capacity. There was, consequently, a remarkable degree of standardisation.

The truly large windows were a feature of later times. Windows were a prominent feature of a mill, but each was comparatively small, the object being to hold within the building the moisture and heat for economic running. The old-time owners also did not wish to see their operatives looking out of the windows; glass was quite often of the "frosted" type.

A mill existed for the making of money; it was plain and utilitarian in the majority of cases, though some mills that rose with outer walls of gleaming Accrington brick were in some measure "show mills", designed partly to impress. Their names reflected the pretentions of the owners, and included *Ace* and *Majestic*. Others indicated strong associations with places overseas where strong trading links existed: *Cairo* and *India*, for example. Generally, the owners who went in for show lost money; their minds were not totally on the business of cotton!

A spinning mill was a considerable employer of labour, and the work force was roughly in balance between men and women. Men were the actual spinners, whereas nearly all the weavers, in sheds to the east, were women. Spinners worked barefooted, on wooden floors, in a temperature maintained between 75 and 98 degrees F. The finer the spinning, and the warmer was the mill. Cotton is at its softest in a high temperature. The operatives were dressed for warm conditions, many having just a "slop" and some being naked from the waist up.

Cotton, prepared for spinning by combing, could then be twisted to make a thread. The world's longest piece of cotton, off the plant, is about $2\frac{1}{2}''$, and the average length used in Lancashire—from cotton imported from America—was about $1\frac{1}{2}''$.

On the spinning side of the industry, the most important change — which was due — came where mule-spinning was replaced by ring-spinning. Crompton's mule-spinner reflected a sound principle, and it provided even, snag-free yarn, but it was bulky and very slow. Some people claim that the mule should never have been invented, being a wildcat concept. One man I met said it gave the impression of having been devised by Heath Robinson, or a man who was at the same time a musician and a carpenter. The width of a mill, of some 100 feet, was fully occupied by the carriage which, set on wheels, twisted the yarn as it moved out and wound the spun yarn on to a cop on its return. Ring-spinning, introduced in the 1890s, but not being fully effective until the late 1920s, involved a stationary machine. The thick thread had its gauge reduced when it was twisted while passing between sets of small rollers of varying speeds. Henceforth, the principal need was a stable building rather than one that was tall and rambling.

In the old days, where medium or short staple cotton was being processed in the cardroom, the air filled with short fibre, known as "fly", and this when inhaled could gravely affect a spinner's health. The mule spinner also suffered from a form of cancer from coming into contact with the oil with which the spindles were lubricated. Ring-spinning demanded from its workers dexterity and obedience: consequently there was an increasing demand for young female labour. From 1932 onwards, British engineering firms came under stiff competition from the Swiss who, until that time, had been content to copy British machines but now made their own to their own designs.

Weaving

A weaving shed was invariably of single storey, with saw-toothed roof lights. Advances in technology that brought in the wide-span roof were not made until after the heyday of cotton manufacture. Anyone moving from a spinning mill to a weaving shed was immediately aware of the dramatic change in noise values. After the "singing" of spinning machinery, a weaving shed was excessively noisy, packed with looms operating from overhead shafts via belting. Before consideration was given to having an adequate space between looms, a person had to walk sideways between whirring belting, wheels and ever-active picking sticks.

No special heating was provided. A shed was often ill-ventilated, with an uncomfortale degree of humidity in deference to the yarn. Each loom once had a gaslight. The gas, turned on at a central point, coursed through considerable lengths of piping while the overlooker walked along the alleys with a taper, lighting the mantles in an atmosphere that was already thick with escaped gas.

Processes associated with weaving are winding and beaming, sizing the thread (traditionally with starch and tallow), twisting and drawing.

Bleaching and Finishing

The bleaching of cloth is an oxydisation process that was first achieved when cloth treated with a variety of simple natural materials, including urine and sour milk, was placed in the sunshine, here to remain for weeks on end. A bleach works is still known as a "croft". The cloth might be bleached in a week through a chlorine process introduced just over a century ago. Now, using peroxide, the bleacher needs only about four hours to complete his work.

Bleaching and finishing were controlled by a relatively small number of large family concerns; the owner frequently lived at a large house standing close to the works. He was always on closer terms with his workers than was the case in spinning and weaving, the main reason being the complexities of finishing cloth and the variety of the products. A small number of workers, all at the craftsman level, was maintained. A firm employing about 300 people might process some half a million yards of cloth a week. To produce that amount of cloth needed the efforts of some 5,000 spinners and 1,000 weavers.

Mill Chimneys

A forest of tall, brick chimneys, breathing dark smoke into the air, testified to the old industrialists that all was well with the world. The earliest chimneys were of stone, square in section.

Then the use of brick, and advances in design, led to the use of lofty, circular chimneys, some of which attained a height of 200 feet. There were still some "show chimneys", notably that at India Mill, Darwen, a place that once specialised in dhotis for the Indian trade. The huge chimney, built in 1870, was made to resemble a Venetian tower, a whim of the owner, who also defied the wind by having the chimney built square in section.

A chimney's height was not just to carry away the smoke and noxious fumes. It was to create a draught for the boiler. Everyone recalled the smoke, however, and in the bad old days some seven tons of soot fell on each square mile of Bolton per annum. At one group of mills, occupying about half a square mile, eight chimneys emitted smoke. At 1 p.m., when the steam pressure was being increased before work resumed at 1·15 p.m., the whole district lay under a dark cloud. Bobs of soot descended on the washing that was hung in back streets to dry.

A firm at Colne is recalled by a man who, in his schooldays, sometimes set off from home as a draught was being put up the chimney, the displaced soot blackening his face. If only one boy turned up at school with a grimy face, he was caned; if there were several the teacher acknowledged that industry was to be blamed. Today, the deposition of soot in central areas of the mill towns is less than a millimetre per annum.

Years ago, when industrial pollution was being discussed at Blackburn, smokeless zones were mentioned. The secretary of the weavers' union, who was more concerned about the shortage of work, said: "Well, I've listened with meticulous particularity with regard to smokeless zones, but, my God, I wish I could see more smoke coming out of our mill chimneys."

Steeplejacks always spoke in yards for measurement. Their employment was potentially dangerous. Comparatively little maintenance was needed apart from attending to the lightning conductor and checking the metal bands set at intervals, but a man might be stranded on top and have to be rescued. A member of an Accrington firm of chimney-builders, though only slight of build, went to the aid of a 16 stone man who was hanging at the top of a chimney, having slipped with one of the coping stones. I met a man who recalled seeing a steeplejack plunging to his death.

Engines and Boilers

Standing near the India Mill at Darwen is a piece of machinery connected with a departing world: a cross compound steam engine that typifies the hundreds of steam engines installed in Lancashire weaving mills from 1830 onwards. This specimen was made at Bolton in 1905, being installed in the following year to power a weaving shed in which there were 1,224 looms. It became obsolete in 1970, and is now preserved. Almost all the mills are now powered by electricity.

The spinning mills, needing the largest engines, used the vertical type, with enormous fly wheel from which extended driving ropes, operating a shaft on each floor. The engine was called upon to operate spinning frames with a length of 100 feet on which spindles revolved at 10,000 revolutions a minute. The swish of ropes up the wallside created a gale inside a mill.

A horizontal type engine was usually sufficient to power a weaving shed, the size and power of the engine being closely related to the number of looms. Details of the engine that can be seen at Darwen are: maximum indicated horse power 450; r.p.m., 75; steam pressure, 125 lb.; stroke length, 3' 6"; high pressure cylinder, 19" dia.; low pressure cylinder, 32" dia.; fly wheel, 15' dia.; ropes, 14 × 1½" dia.; weight of fly wheel, 8 tons 2 cwt. 9 lb.; shaft diameter 12".

The engineer at a mill formed a considerable affection for his engine, which usually had the name of a woman. It was known for hard-faced men to weep when the mill at which they had worked for years went under the hammer and their precious steam engines were sold. The engineer, a dedicated man, attended the mill early and returned after the normal day's work to stoke up the boiler. He was respected by all, including the boss. He responded by keeping his engine in such a perfect state that one might balance on it a sixpence, standing on end. That, at least, was the claim.

When the big engine stopped at dinnertime, a donkey engine continued to serve the tape room, where the process of sizing the yarn prior to weaving must be maintained. The engineer synchronised the speeds of the respective engines to such perfection that as one stopped the other took over with scarcely a jolt. With the use of electrical power, group drives were possible in a weaving shed. Eventually a small motor was fitted to each loom. The line shafts and belting were now obsolete, to the relief of the weavers.

The Lancashire boiler made good steam—and plenty of smoke. One boiler that is still being used in a mill of moderate size near Blackburn is 120 feet long, with a diameter of nine feet and a capacity of 30,000 gallons. It is notable for its constancy; the engineer can leave it for a while without attention and in the knowledge that it will hold its pressure. Typically, it has twin fireboxes and incorporates a means of pre-heating the water.

Fuel for the fire is gravity fed from hoppers. In the old days, the fires were stoked directly by hand, with extra large shovels. At week-ends, prior to "dampening down", the fireman made a bright fire and then added wet coal, at the same time cutting off the main draught. When work ended at dinnertime on Saturday, excess steam was released. The malfunction of an injector pump on the boiler of a Blackburn mill led to an empty boiler. The engineer, instead of raking out the fire, turned in fresh water. The covers of the boiler, blown through the roof, were never found.

At another mill, in Nelson, the mill engine did not stop at breakfast-time. Someone went to the engine house and discovered that the engineer had died when his jacket caught the belting as he oiled the main shaft, and he was dragged round.

As the engine of a mill began its work, workers heard a reluctant growl from the gearing; the growl increased in volume and became a low roar. Leather belting, some two inches wide, was unguarded, and many workers, especially girls with long hair, were injured. "Mop caps" were introduced at about the time of the 1914-18 war.

The Lancashire Loom: It has been termed a "blacksmith's job" — a relatively simple, unsophisticated machine, the main parts of which are derived from rough castings. The technique of the Lancashire, or non-automatic, loom was that established in the handloom days, and the three main principles were shuttle flight, shedding (the changing direction of the thread) and the beat-up. The sequence of activity is repeated about 200 times a minute. I was told: "Anyone who looked at a Lancashire loom could understand the rudiments of weaving; you saw everything. I still like listening to the clatter of looms though, to be fair, I don't have to listen to it all day. To me, it's a merry sound."

The Lancashire loom has served the industry well. Comparatively little modification to the basic design has been needed. It will go on weaving a fault continuously, however, until the error is corrected. The automatic loom stops when a thread breaks. In the production of a standard cloth, the Lancashire loom is capable of weaving about eight yards in eight hours. The picking-stick, which is responsible for most of the clatter in the shed, projects the shuttle from one side of the loom to another, simulating the movement of a human arm.

The Lancashire loom was hard on weavers. Its clatter affected their hearing. Old-timers lost their two front teeth through "kissing the shuttle", or sucking the thread into the eye, a process that became obsolete when shuttles were devised so that thread could be inserted by hand. In the days of shuttle-kissing, much dirty fluff entered the mouth of an operator.

Mill Fires

Spinning mills, their wooden floors impregnated with oil, were notable fire hazards. A six-storey mill could burn itself out in an hour. The fire risk was particularly high in the days when gas provided illumination, but the operatives of a spinning mill were outstanding as fire-fighters. Even before the fire brigade could be alerted, a mule-spinner and his staff had the measure of the outbreak, using buckets and brushes. They knew every trick to keep a fire under control.

Cotton fluff was oily, as well as fluffy, being at times almost explosive. The largest conflagrations were nearly always caused by operatives smoking in lavatories. They carried matches, some of which were inclined to be dropped. If a non-safety match fell on to cotton which was then passed through a machine, a serious fire could result.

In a weaving shed, the floor and machinery were cleaned by the operatives during the last half hour of the working week; in later years, men were employed to do this. Sometimes, as the overlooker used a taper to ignite the gas lighting, the "dawn" would ignite and fire would spread along a line of looms. The weavers whacked the flames with any suitable piece of material. Smoking was prohibited in the tape room because the risk of fire here was particularly high.

Maisters

IN the early days, a strong family interest pervaded the upper levels of the cotton industry. By the 1930s, when there were many amalgamations, the homely touch was being lost. The old Lancashire saying, "clogs to clogs in three generations", could be a remarkably accurate assessment of the ownership of a business. The founder was usually a talented man. He could not be other than a successful boss. His son carried on the work, but frequently the third generation was brought up "soft" and could not stand the hurly-burly of mill administration. They desired a well-paid job, with membership of the Manchester Exchange, a railway contract, and opportunities to play golf.

Employers in the spinning area included tough businessmen— operatives who, even if they became bosses, did not try to improve their cultural level, their behaviour, manners or attitude to life. Their like might be seen in Oldham or Rochdale; they have been represented in the classic plays about Lancashire mill life. In the Bolton area, the type of employer was more gentlemanly and may, indeed, have been a gentleman before becoming a boss. He maintained family traditions of high culture. Sir Ben Dobson, of Dobson and Barlow, which had strong associations with the textile trade, was a literary man who was also qualified scientifically. Making machinery for the mills, he offered products that were well ahead of their time and sold them remarkably cheaply. He rejoiced as much in evolutionary creation as in making a profit.

The weaving boss was usually a man who had been a weaver himself and had made good. To be effective, he had usually to have experienced the noisy workings of the shed. B. Bowker, looking back to the opulent years from 1900 to the start of the 1914-18 war, recalled that "any man who could tell or be taught the difference between healds and reeds, who could rake together a few hundreds of capital and rent some room and power, and who could also get a friend to show him the ropes on 'Change (the Manchester Cotton Exchange) was made. With ordinary care for a dozen years, he would be able to retire to a mansion at Southport, or a village on the Blackpool coast. Indeed, with the barest trifle more than usual luck, he might meet his ambition half way by living at St. Annes and being borne, godlike, each day to Manchester on a 'club' express which no ordinary mortal might enter."

Another story related by Bowker concerned a weaver who, in 1908, married the daughter of a manufacturer, sold yarn at a half per cent commission on 'Change, became an independent yarn agent, and in 1912 moved to a fine house at Southport. By 1920, he had £150,000 and had bought a yet bigger house at St. Annes.

Success stories were numerous (as were also stories of businesses that failed). Bowker mentioned a middle-aged man who in 1903 kept a small shop; he entered the cotton trade with money bequeathed to him by his father. He first arranged with the village schoolmaster to teach him the rudiments of mathematics, and then he became master of 600 looms, beginning a leisured Indian summer of retirement with £50,000. This man had luckily entered the business in 1920, during the industry's last great fling before its steady decline. He got out before the crash.

Weaving bosses are often recalled as being "stingy". In the late 1920s, the owner of a small firm in Colne throve on commission work. He lived at a big house on the edge of town, yet walked to work, making a point of arriving before 7 a.m., at which time the door of the mill was locked. Any weaver who was late for work had to stand outdoors until it was re-opened half an hour later. This boss wore a bowler hat as a mark of status; he appeared to despise his workforce, and when one of them complained of poor-quality yarn and said that before she wove any more she would "gie ower first", he replied: "Tha wean't. Tha can't afford." He was right, for she was the family's only wage-earner, her father being absent and her mother ill. The mill-owner treated representatives of the union with disdain, or he threatened to have them thrown down the steps of the office.

Up to the 1930s, a mill-owner tended not to show weakness before his workers. Yet if a weaver stood up to him, he often thought of it as being a measure of character rather than a personal affront. Mill-owners could be considerate, even generous, to those who had worked for them for years. Christian names were used. A man might make a point of walking round each department of the mill daily, having a few words with each operative.

Life was quite good for bosses until about the 1914-18 war. A mill town community had, at the peak of its social pyramid, the boss, then the magistrate, doctor and policeman. A schoolteacher was lower down, on a par with ministers of religion, and at the bottom was the grey mass of working people. After the war came disillusionment with the social fabric, and also such difficult times that now a boss feared for his livelihood.

A typical mill office block had three rooms — one for the manager, one in which a staff of two or three people did the clerical work (it also held the large safe containing all the account books), and an inner sanctum, the preserve of the mill-owner and his son. This inner room was usually carpeted and held a good quality desk and several chairs of more than utilitarian appearance. Yet a mill office at Nelson was described by a former clerk as like a large hen hut, no more, standing in a corner of the mill. Within that hut, the boss had his corner, and other members of the staff had their corners. It was a spartan place. A pull-handle adding machine was the only modern device, and the operator could usually add up faster in his head than through working the machine. The clerks sat at Bob Cratchit-type stools. Tall desks were bought second-hand from firms that had gone bankrupt. The toilets were outside in the yard.

The owner of this Nelson mill is recalled as a man who was thrifty to the point of stinginess. The office boy had to be at work at 6-50 a.m. to light the gas mantles. After a new boy had been working for several months, he was summoned by the boss, who opened a drawer of his desk and produced a tobacco tin in which were small pieces of taper. They had been taken from the waste paper basket. When the boy protested that they were too short to be held, the boss patiently explained: "Thou sticks a pin in t'bottom an' then holds it up to t'gas. We don't waste tapers here."

Servility was practised by many weavers, but some could show genuine hatred of the boss. A contract weaver of the late 1920s fined his workers if a fault occurred: if, for example, a weaver had "an end down" above four inches. The fine, usually sixpence, was deducted from the wage—"he didn't even say, 'you owe me sixpence'." This weaver had the satisfaction of finding better work elsewhere. She was determined never to return to the old weaving shed. On the last day of employment, she collected her wages, tracked down the boss and told him exactly what she thought of him. She then asked to see his two sons in turn, and they too were rebuked.

It was customary in those days for the sons of a mill boss to be called by their Christian name—preceded by the respectful term "Mr.". Before the 1914-18 war, some bosses expected their workers to raise their hats to him if they met him in the street after work. A Blackburn electrician whose girl friend worked at a local mill in the early 1930s one day rang up the mill and asked to speak to her. He was told: "We don't have weavers in our office."

Anyone talking to workpeople will not expect to hear good words about the boss, of course. More respect was shown to the bosses by the overlookers, or tacklers. At Burnley, a tackler called Jim Catlow, who was president of the Overlookers' Association, frequently met a local employer called John Gray. He was knighted. At the first meeting following the investiture, the tackler said: "Good morning, Sir John." He replied: "Now, Jim, it's always been Jim and John between thee and me, and that's th'way it's going to go on."

At one Blackburn mill the owner's brother was the manager and his two sons were a taper and office worker. The family thus maintained close and homely terms with the employees. A mother who took her daughter to the mill asked him if there was a job for her. The owner put his arm round the mother and said to the daughter: "If tha'rt awf as good at weyvin' as thi mother wur, tha'll do."

The Boss at Home

Amos Nelson started work as a half-timer and became a man of such wealth that he could have his business in the town of Nelson and develop an estate at West Marton. More than this, he was able to have the old hall demolished and to instruct Sir Edwin Lutyens to design him a new one, complete with lodges. The new Gledstone Hall followed the theme of Lutyens—the old English barn—and among its features was a grand staircase with alternating white and black marble steps.

At one time, cotton money sustained palatial homes like castles in Cumbria and North Lancashire. Every mill town had its high-class residential district, where lived the wealthier mill-owners and their families, but nearly every mill-owner had in his mind the thought of retiring to a villa at St. Annes or Southport.

The old-time boss did not want to appear to lord it over his workers; he could be frugal in his relations with the mill, but opulent in his private life. He wanted to appear prosperous in the eyes of the townsfolk without being showy. Quite often, a mill-owner had a background of devout nonconformity, and though he lived well he kept his private life under restraint. Others joined the "hunting and shooting" set.

The good years provided funds for the construction of large houses to replace the more modest mill-owner homes that stood near the mills. Many of the new houses were Georgian in character, with broad steps leading to the front door and tiling in the hall of mosaic. The best of furniture, and potted ferns, decked the main rooms. A billiards room was often a feature, its importance being not just for recreation. Here was a place to which the men could retire for serious talk. A mansion on the edge of Blackburn is recalled because of the beauty of the candelabra in the dining room and the presence in the big lounge of an expensive pianola. The principal bedrooms occupied the first floor, with tiny rooms for the servants at the top of the house. A system of bells enabled the owner or his family to summon servants instantly.

In winter, some of these houses paid for their fine elevated positions by being cut off after heavy snowfalls. A Nelson mill-owner is remembered by a former clerk because of the mornings when, at about 7-15 a.m., he rang up the office and told the boy to approach the office manager at 8 a.m. The manager must get threepence from the safe. The boy should collect a shovel from the engine shed, use the money to travel by bus and clear the drive leading to the big house so that the owner could drive to work. When the task was done, the owner would drive off, saying to the clerk: "Thee catch bus wi' that three-orpence tha's got left!"

Manchester Men

The cotton industry had its temple. It was known as the Manchester Cotton Exchange, abbreviated to 'Change. Here the spinner could meet the supplier of raw cotton and, within a minute or two of selling some yarn, order fresh supplies of the precise type required. A weaver could go to the spinner and ask what price was being demanded for a specific weight and quality of yarn. All the important men went to 'Change. It was thus possible for transactions to be virtually simultaneous. A man with a good memory did not even make a note of the transactions; he would jot down the details when he returned to the office. It was known for a man to record details of transactions when he returned from holiday.

By its size and dignity, 'Change reflected the state of the industry in the heady years up to the 1914-18 war. Well remembered are two mottoes that were displayed in large, ornate letters. In a cupola that from the inside looked like the dome of St. Paul's was the inscription: "Who seeks to find eternal treasure, should use no guile in weight or measure." This had its humour in the cotton trade, where a fair amount of guile was used—and understood by the different interests. The other motto was: "A good name is rather to be chosen than great riches, and living favour rather than silver and gold."

Great pillars were a feature of the Cotton Exchange, and a man might arrange to meet his customers opposite a specific pillar, say D.12. A man was allowed to take along visitors three times a year, but he must record their presence at the entrance. The sellers of several companies wore top hats, partly to distinguish them from the others, who usually had bowler hats or trilbies. When some of the younger men began to attend 'Change showing bared heads, the elders reacted with horror.

From 10 a.m. the changing prices of cotton in Liverpool were revealed on an ingenious board on the wall. The figures changed every few seconds as they reacted to changing conditions of trade. Business ended at 4 p.m. The cotton market was sophisticated. A man could make or lose a fortune when buying or selling "futures".

People living in the mill towns watched the departure of the Manchester Men with some envy. In the earlier days, the owners arrived at the station in horse-drawn carriages; later they would have the most fashionable cars. On Tuesdays and Fridays, the merchants and representatives of the bleachers and dyers were in attendance. The latter had no direct orders to place, but they were anxious to find out what was imminent in production. They could also discuss with the merchants and others any problems that had occurred in the finishing.

In Nelson and Colne, where some wool was processed, a manufacturer or his representative might attend two Exchanges —in Manchester and Bradford.

Operatives

A WOMAN at Blackburn told me: "We taught them how to weave. Now they've taken our trade from us." *They* were the competitors overseas. In meeting the world's demand for cotton goods, the old-time textile operatives worked a day shift only. When, in recent years, the manufacturers—having invested in new machinery—requested work in shifts round the clock, the new system was actually welcomed by women, who could spend this part of each day with their children.

The industry was complex, but a number of general categories might be described:

The Overlooker. He has been long known as the tackler, and he is still a power in the mill. He ensures that the machinery in his charge is running efficiently. The former manager of a spinning mill in Bolton told me that men who became tacklers were engineers of such quality that they were able to instantly improve the performance of machines as they were delivered from the manufacturers by tuning them to the mill's special requirements. In a weaving shed, a tackler once maintained a specific number of looms. There might be as many as 160 in his charge, his wages being assessed on every £1 earned by the weavers, which gave him a considerable interest in their efficiency. The situation was summed up by a Burnley man: "If a tackler wasn't working, everything was grand. If a weaver wasn't working, she was getting the top rate for the job. The harder you worked, and the less you earned!"

A man became a tackler after being a weaver for some years. He then did some odd-jobbing. The jobs handed out by an established tackler included assembling parts for a broken loom or replacing a beam. The best men became tacklers when in their early twenties, and a tackler's job was secure and well-paid.

He was a man with an aptitude for improvisation. No two looms were alike. One would demand a heavier weight at the back, to keep up the tension, than did its neighbour. Another, with a peculiarity, needed to be wedged. Tacklers had their own little room, or bench or they would sit in the tape room. A weaver who had trouble with a loom sought out the tackler. When the difficulty was explained, the tackler might say: "Which loom? Fourth from th'end. Aye. I know about it. It'll be *that* wheel." He went and did what was required.

A Burnley man recalls that before the 1914-18 war all the tacklers wore white fustian trousers. They were not allowed to smoke in the mill, and so they chewed tobacco. About the middle 1920s he noticed a change in their appearance. Every self-respecting tackler wore a moustache, but suddenly there was a fashion for being clean-shaven. "It got to be quite a craze. A man would slip off to the barbers to have his moustache snipped off."

As in all professions, there were good, bad and indifferent workers. If a weaver had a bad tackler, he moaned. There would be a lot of extra work. "When you thought the tackler was at fault, you just turned round and gave him a few sharp words!" A mill manager says: "Tacklers were not appreciated as they should have been. With the Lancashire loom, all depended on his skill and know-how. He had to feel for the correct delivery of cloth. He had to be sensitive to the proper flight of the shuttle. The automatic loom of today knocks the shuttle across, but with the Lancashire loom the shuttle is slung from a leather sling, offering a movement that's smooth and beautiful—if all is well."

A Nelson weaver remembers a special cabin provided for tacklers. The cabin had a rough wood table, with a piece of oil-cloth to cover the working surface. The old-time tackler had to be nimble as he carried a warp to the loom, dodging belts and then, dropping on one knee, getting the beam into position. It was impossible to wheel-in a beam because the space between looms was constricted.

A weaver with only four looms was aware of impending faults before a breakdown occurred. The tackler could keep abreast of the work. "When they put her on 12 looms, she'd not see that anything was unusual until part of the machine dropped off!" A man who recalled the tacklers as "generally a surly lot" mentioned an element of indifference. "A tackler would come if he felt like it. There were often slanging matches between tacklers and weavers. You'd hear a weaver say: 'It's banging up, and it's been banging up for the last ten minutes.' The tackler would reply: 'I'll come when I've a minute!' The weaver would retort:

'If you don't get off your bottom I'll have nowt to draw at weekend'." If the weft would not leave the shuttle, a weaver would knock on the door of the tackler's cabin and say: "Mi loom's weaving baht weft!"

A new-starter in a weaving shed was told by her mother: "Go an' tell tackler the monkey's tail's loose." She did so, expecting to be ridiculed. "I thought he'd laugh at me, but he didn't. He came and tightened up the monkey's tail!"

The tackler was the butt on many jokes. So popular did tacklers' tales become that some of them were printed on match-boxes. "He was not supposed to be quite all there." The wife of a tackler acquired a new clothes prop, but there was no notch at the top. The tackler asked his wife to hold up the prop in the backyard while he went to a bedroom window. Leaning out, he grasped the end of the prop and sawed a notch! A new tackler who went round the mill to check on the number of defective gas mantles returned to the manager and said that the figure was 896. He had tested each of them; they were all soft!

A tackler who kept some hens on spare ground decided to dispose of them and, instead, to acquire some pigeons. He sold the hen hut. Lads from the mill helped to carry the hut to its new owner. One of them protesting at the weight found that the tackler was crouching inside the hut, carrying the perches!

Here are some classical tackler tales:

A tackler's wife was lying ill in bed. The doctor ordered a powder to be administered, and the husband was asked to give her a dose sufficient to cover a sixpenny piece. When the wife did not improve, he explained: "I hadn't sixpence. I gave her t'stuff on five pennies and two haw-pennies." A Pendleton man called at the butcher's and ordered a tackler (also the name for a sheep's head). When it was collected, the customer objected to its size. "Tha doesn't mean to say as that's a tackler?" "Neaw," replied the butcher, "but it will be when I've taken brains out."

A Bolton tackler had just bought a modern house. A coal merchant asked him if he could supply him with coal. "Nay, lad, aw'se not wantin' coal. There's hot and cowd watter i' every slopstone." A party of tacklers visited a Blackpool cafe, and one poured his tea into the saucer in the usual way. His neighbour nudged him. "Sam, lad, drink out o' thi cup." Sam replied: "I cornd. Blooming spoon's in t'way."

The tackler had to administer the unpopular slate system, by which the details of each weaver's weekly earnings were displayed for all to see. He was also often abused for what was in reality the employer's keenness to get maximum profits by way of "time-cribbing", under which the mill engine was started up a little before the official commencement of the working day and was allowed to run beyond the customary time for closure.

Spinners and Weyvers. Cotton production was sustained by an army of workers. In the spinning mills, there was greater parity between men and women; the dominant need in the weaving shed was for women. The influence the mill exerted on a family is illustrated by that of a Bolton man, now retired after many years of mill managership. His father was one of a family of eight, all of whom worked in the spinning mills. The family tradition continued: "As a manager, I found that if I was rough with one person, I had also been rough with 10 or 12 people—the other members of his family!" It was the height of working class luxury when the mother did not need to go out to work.

Mill profits depended largely on the nearby presence of a large and inexpensive labour force, a proportion of which consisted of children. The half-timer, known as a tenter, spent part of his or her day at school and part of it amid the clatter of a mill. "My sister was a half-timer," I was told by a woman at Colne. "One week she went to the mill in the morning; next week, she was there in the afternoon. The rest of the time was spent at school. She started at six o'clock and had a long green card that was marked to show she had been to both places. She'd be 12 years old at the time." The age at which juvenile labour might be employed in the mills was raised from 11 to 12 as recently as 1900. Half-time working for children under 14 was abolished under the Education Act, 1918, though the provision did not actually come into practice until 1921.

A woman born in 1896 had been taught how to weave by the time she was 13 years old; she was never a half-timer. "My parents showed me how to weave; it took them about four months. Then I started by myself on two looms." The workings of the tenter system were explained by a former Colne weaver, who said: "If you'd a child who wanted to learn to weave, the man or lady who took you—it was usually a man—would get another loom. You had to help him. Once you got going, you'd get a few shillings a week, and he'd try to make some profit out of you. He'd have you sweeping and doing the other dirty jobs. In my time, the late 1920s, I've seen a man kick a tenter. There was a girl who lived near us, and if she didn't just do as quick as the weaver thought, he'd just kick her. Some men were nice; some were rotten."

She was fortunate, and was taught by her mother. "Then eventually I got two looms at the side of her. When you learnt to weave, you worked for nothing. Mother was losing money, because she had to stop her looms when she showed me anything. It would be about six months after I started that I got two looms."

In the days when children left school at 13, a so-called medical inspection was carried out before work in a mill could begin.

A Burnley man recalls: "You went to the doctor. You stood in front of him, and he looked you down. Then he looked at your teeth. He signed a certificate that you were fit for work." This man, recalling his first days in the mill, told me he was out of bed at 5-30 and commenced work at 6 a.m. As a child of 13, he went round the shed lighting the gas-burners. "Fancy, a kid of 13 doing this." He then made the rounds collecting the breakfast cans of the men, slipping the cans on hooks driven into a long piece of wood. The cans had to be filled with hot water for the eight o'clock brew-up. The rest of the day was spent in "carrying and fetching," and with a handcart he delivered items about the town. "Once, when I'd a big load, a man said to the boss: 'Eh, Bill, tha shouldn't have a lad shoving a cart like that.' Boss said: 'Oh, it's all reight. Some silly blighter 'll give 'im a push if 'e needs it.'"

A man who, as a lad in Oswaldtwistle, ran errands for the mill, using a bicycle, went to Blackburn to collect castings but he was told at the office that he would have to wait for them. He sat in the yard, on some old weft boxes, and a manager passed. "How much a week are you getting?" asked the manager, to be told: "Seven and six, sir." He took the lad to the office, told a clerk to give him 7s. 6d. and then showed him off the premises. When he returned to the place where he actually worked, his explanation was received with merriment—and he was allowed to keep the money.

Another half-timer, during a breakfast break, decided that the looms were working too slowly. He borrowed a spanner from the tackler's bench and changed the gearing. The mill engine resumed. The loom went at a cracking speed, and the half-timer was proud of his achievement, though he did notice that the cloth was coming off as thin as bandaging. Everyone, including the tackler, stared at the loom in amazement. The tackler brought the manager. The half-timer proudly admitted what he had done. He was sacked—more or less. His mother was told: "This is no place for him."

The daily routine for many spinners and weavers began with the knocker-up. Alice Foley, of Bolton, has written: "Each morning, at four o'clock he started on his rounds carrying a long pole crowned with a bunch of umbrella wires; with this he tapped on the front bedroom windows, waking sleepers and calling out the time of day. On inclement days, the knocker-up gave warning to his customers—'bad mornin', 'cold', 'foggy' or 'slippy'; sleepy voices called back 'aa reet'. For this cheerful, punctual service he received fourpence a week from each household."

Quite often, the knocker-up was an old-age pensioner, as small and as thin as were the wires on top of his pole. He applied the wire against a bedroom window as though it was a percussion instrument. At one house, he might bounce the wires up and down, creating a tattoo. If he twirled it—and he could do it with verve—the whirring sound was calculated to waken up someone in the next street.

The knocker-up did not move on until he was convinced he had been heard. There had to be an acknowledgement from within the house. A paper blind would be rolled up, and a rapping heard as the sleepy occupant of a bedroom applied a knuckle to the glass. Or the knocker-up would see the bedroom become faintly illuminated as the gas on the wall bracket spluttered into life.

The morning serenade was romanticised in a novel by Allen Clark, in 1896: "Dick spoke. 'The town's getting up to its work,' he said, 'though I'm afraid most of the older folks are grumbling at having to rise, and the younger ones are being dragged out of bed. Hark, the hideous steam buzzers are beginning to shriek. The knockers-up are busy rattling at the windows; the toilers surlily jump up and tap back at the pane, growling 'What, time to get up already? I'm sure I've nobbut just come to bed. Eh, I could just do wi' another turn o'er.' They are spluttering about in the dark, shivering as they stick their legs into icy trousers and skirts, and wishing the factories were at the bottom of the sea. In a few minutes the streets will be full of the great glum procession hurrying to the mills and workshops."

A Nelson man said that even in the early 1930s, when both his parents were weavers, they left to go to work for 7 a.m. "From about 6-40 until 7 we got this terrific sound of clog irons on the paving stones as the workers clomped up to the mills. It reached a crescendo about 10 minutes before work was due to start, and then it began to tail off. But there were always the latecomers, running in their clogs towards the mill gates."

In the decade before the 1914-18 war, the sound of clogs against flagstones seemed to make the towns tremble. A Foulridge weaver who was busy in the mill at that time remembers that the working day began at 6 a.m. She arose at 5-30 to make cups of tea for members of her family. "You could hear clogs clanking away all over the village." Half an hour was allowed for breakfast, from 8 a.m.

When members of a family went to work at different times, and a house had only one key—usually a large mortice lock key—it was customary for the first man out to lock the door and push the key through the letterbox. One day, it was said, a woman knocked up the others in the house and, in great dismay, asked them to pick up the key and throw it out to her. She had forgotten to lock the door!

A Burnley man whose memories of life at the begnning of this century have been richly augmented by what an aunt told him of earlier times, relates that she worked from the age of nine until her 66th birthday. Only once was she late for work. The overlooker stood on the doorstep and told her: "St. John's clock is striking six, go home!" As late as the 1920s, a worker who was only fractionally late might have his job taken over by one of the sad little queue of people—the "tramp weavers"—gathering at the mill gate. A Colne woman relates: "If you weren't at the mill just before seven, the doors were locked. You were kept out in the cold until 7-30." A weaver dare not miss turning up; she would lose her looms.

The law eventually allowed a weaver to be off work on Saturday from noon. The mill gates remained closed until the last moment. The last half hour of the week was devoted to cleaning and sweeping. "If a person finished early, he or she had to wait until the clock chimed before going home."

Memories remain fresh of the early morning walks to work. A woman who lived at Brierfield and worked at Colne had a particularly awkward journey, accomplished in part by bus. She clambered out of bed at 5-30 and walked down to catch a bus at 6-20. The bus took her to Nelson. There followed another bus ride and a walk of about a quarter of an hour to the mill, which she reached just before 7 a.m.

The Weaver's Lot. A weaver remembers in particular the winter days when, with hardly any heating, the shed was like a refrigerator. "There was just enough heat to keep the yarn happy," says a Colne woman. In the cold, the ends kept dropping down. I used to dread it. Everything was cold, and your hands were soon cold because everything about a Lancashire loom was made of iron. You could hardly tie knots because your hands were frozen. If you got wet through on the way to work, you stayed wet. There was nowhere to go to change your clothes or dry off."

A Foulridge weaver remembers when weavers stopped their looms and left the mill after complaining about the cold. The owner said he would not provide more steam because of the cost. He threatened to "shop" their looms, making them available to others. One of the women who went home told me of the arrival, shortly afterwards, of the warehouseman, who repeated the boss's threat to "shop" the looms. The weavers stayed out until next morning. On their return, their looms were still available.

Weavers stood in their clogs on the stone flags and, with chattering teeth, applied themselves to work. They were paid on piece rates. "You used to dread winter work," says a retired weaver at Colne. "The light was that poor, even after they'd turned on the gas. You'd see a tackler coming with a new warp. If it had black on it, you dreaded working with it. I've known a weaver take a bicycle lamp to work with her so she could see to take the ends up."

The old-time weaver was clad in a blouse and long skirt over which was spread a "warkin' brat", or apron. She had a belt, with a pouch for the main tools of her trade—reed hook, comb and scissors. She operated the loom, collected weft from the store, carried pieces to the warehouse, swept and cleaned the machinery. Those working for firms who did commission weaving usually had poor quality yarn. A Colne weaver recalls: "If stuff was poor it wouldn't stand a lot of rubbing through the reed. Ends were always coming down and making a float (fault)." The weaver had to continually "pull back".

Floats were the weaver's responsibility. They were detected when the cloth went to the warehouse. The cut-looker examined every inch and if a blemish was found the warehouse lad was sent into the shed to summon the offending weaver. As the lad appeared, everyone kept an eye on him. Whom would he approach? A tap on a shoulder, and a flustered woman followed the lad to have her weaving error pointed out. As if she needed to be told! A Blackburn man says: "I've seen teenage girls weeping as the cut-looker gave them some rough language." The process of being summoned to the warehouse was known to the weavers as being "fetched up". An old-style manufacturer of Colne, known for his broad speech, said: "Nah then; what's ta bin doin'?" There was a pause, and he added: "I'll fine thee a tanner."

Meanwhile, the weaver hoped that the other looms would continue to work correctly while she was away. The week's pay depended entirely on production. If a float occurred, a weaver had to weigh up the extent of a calamity. Was it worth while to pull back the cloth or not? A weaver was noted for her dexterity in repairing a certain type of fault. Her set of looms would be kept running by the person who had quietly summoned her to camouflage the flaw.

And so they wove cloth, throughout the long days, amid the clatter of a shed, with belts whirring dangerously around them. Constant leaning over a loom would wear out the pinafore. A weaver would attach to it a fent to protect her clothing.

The manager of a firm where the Lancashire loom is still employed said: "We'd amaze you what we can do with cloth." One day he was passing through the shed when a young weaver complained that her loom was running slowly. An older weaver, standing across the alley, said: "It's not the loom's fault. The shed's too wet." Indeed, the yarn was so moist it was slowing down the loom. "I turned the moisture down, and within half an hour the loom was operating at normal speed." Some weavers prided themselves on being able to throw the shuttle. "We went on to a system for which we had to check on the work-rate of the weavers. When the figures for one woman were prepared, the experts said it was not possible for her to have woven so much. So they stood over her and watched her work. At the change of shuttle, the loom did not actually stop; she'd knock the handle off as a shuttle was virtually empty, and the loom would continue to turn over. As the shuttle came across, she took it off and put in another, setting the loom in operation before its working parts came to a standstill."

Weavers who worried about the dryness of the shed in summer, threw water underneath the loom to humidify the warp. "Or they'd get thrums—a number of ends—and saturate them with water. The thrums were put across the top of the loom so that they actually touched the warp, which was kept moist." Small areas that had been missed in the earlier sizing process would be rubbed with an old tallow candle or even a bar of soap. If there was a fault caused when the threads did not interlace, the shed's specialist would be consulted. Later, the cloth-looker would remark to a friend: "Maggie's good at dressing a float." He recognised an individual's effort. "Nowadays, they call the process invisible mending," said a mill manager.

A stranger, entering an old-style weaving shed, was immediately aware of the noise; it reached a level sufficient to induce pain. An operative became accustomed to it. Selective hearing was possible. A retired weaver told me: "Amid all that din I could actually hear the threads passing the reed, and the shuttle passing the threads. I could hear the arrival and departure of the shuttle. You'd hear nothing. It'd just be a deafening roar to you."

The problem of a noisy shed was overcome by the Lancashire weaver's ability to lip-read, which is known locally as "mee-mawing". A good weaver could converse with a friend across the shed without uttering a sound. Mee-mawing worked as fast as you could think. Enter a shed, and you would hear a sound like *whoo,* as a weaver attracted another's attention. The message would quickly spread. The hands of a clock were imitated by the use of fingers. A weaver would say something, then pause until the other person nodded, signifying that the message was understood.

The clatter stopped at 11-30 a.m. on Saturday for the week-end break. "We stopped weaving and started sweeping, using a fairly long-handled brush. We tackled the cranks, then the wheels, then went round the back of the loom, and finished by sweeping the front. The boss walked round and he'd say: 'There's a bit o' dawn there—you'd better have another poke'."

In later times, sweepers and oilers were employed. The sweeping was carried out partly to reduce the fire risk. "If anyone dropped a light on the down, it went up whoosh! If you didn't oil properly, and something got hot, your looms were aflame. You were responsible. You'd missed oiling. If we went into the country, we'd pick up hen feathers." A trimmed feather, dipped in a little oil, was applied to the more delicate parts of the loom.

Dangers to Health. Steaming a shed kept the humidity high but created an unhealthy atmosphere for the workers. The Medical Officer of Health for Blackburn commented sternly on the disadvantages of "steaming" as far back as 1887. The borough health committee instituted a special inquiry in 1888, and it reported a year later. A petition, presented to Parliament, signed by nearly 220,000 people, urged that the abuses of "steaming" should end. Not until 1929 were the recommendations now in force given legal backing.

Weavers coughed when inhaling an irritant dust from the sizes used for warps—sizes that contained zinc chloride. They coughed when their mouths and, ultimately, their lungs were infected with fluff from "kissing the shuttle", a practice that continued until the shuttle was modified so that it could be threaded easily by hand. "Kissing" involved sucking the thread through a hole.

The flying shuttle was feared. A shuttle, streamlined and with pointed metal ends, occasionally left a loom, travelling at some 40 feet a second. It could inflict terrible injuries. A weaver said: "I got a whacker on my arms and ribs. I'd just set my looms on in the morning, and was still half asleep. I wondered what had hit me." Weavers showed me old wounds on wrist and face; one was about half an inch from an eye.

On a lighter note, I heard from a Nelson man about the day he was told to take a tray of poppies through the shed just before Armistice Day. He realised that the picking stick was potentially injurious when one caught his tray, sending it and the poppies into the air. "The shed seemed full of flying poppies. Some fell on the looms and were woven into the cloth!"

Rates for the Job. There was no standard rate of pay until quite recent times. A weaver was on piece rates, and these varied from mill to mill, sometimes within a single mill. In hard times some weavers were persuaded to accept a return lower than the agreed rate, and when the mill operated on short time they would be given job priority. A uniform list of rates of pay was actually introduced in 1892. At that time the round figure of 20s. a week was being paid to a weaver in the Manchester area. The average wage of a weaver in Preston in 1906 was 19s. 5d. and in Black-burn 22s. 1d. Two years later, the average in north-east Lan-cashire was between 23s. 8d. and 24s.

A census of weavers' earnings in 1913 revealed an average of 6s. 6⅞d. per loom or 26s. 3½d. per week for a weaver with four looms. The average weaver earned 31s. 5d. in 1936, and two years later it was 36s. 8d. Wages were usually collected at the ware-house but a Colne weaver recalled that at her shed on pay day the tackler toured the shed with a tray on which were small tin cups, each having the number of a loom. The cups held the wages. The cash was tipped into the hands of the employees.

The Union.   Nelson became known as Little Moscow. It was here, in the 1930s, that impressive marches took place to draw attention to the poor wage rate of weavers. Generally, the textile workers were not very well organised or demonstrative, and in the early days of the unions a worker who became actively associated with a union might be threatened with dismissal. Some employers acted tersely, sometimes even roughly, towards union representatives.

Yet the unions worked valiantly to improve working condi-tions. As far back as 1896, when the millfolk at Barnoldswick struck, and employers imported strangers to replace the lost labour, the union spent £850 a week in maintaining the strike.

A former tackler recalls: "Some people say that workers in the textile trade gave little trouble, but believe me they had their moments." When the industry was feeling the pinch about 1932, operatives were asked to put back half-a-crown in the £ they drew in wages. "Some mills were going on short time. I remember that a lot of weavers had only one loom instead of four. People tend to forget there were a lot of strikes about that time."

The *Rules* of the Darwen Weavers', Winders' and Warpers' Association, revised in 1892, reflected the general desire to improve the workers' income with the words: "It is pleasant and cheering to reflect that within recent years a better feeling has sprung up, that the repulsive power of isolation has melted away before the genial influences of union, and as a consequence the precarious system of wages, which was formerly the curse of operatives, has well nigh disappeared, and something like a uniform rate of wages has been obtained; although it is not contended that anything like perfection has been secured."

There was a pride in the various unions on the part of craft workers — overlookers, twisters and drawers, the tape-sizers, warehouse personnel, weavers and cardroom workers. (The spinners and cardroom workers had merged.) All the unions cherished their local autonomy. A union official remarked: "We are still very proud of it. If there is a dispute at any of the mills, it can be discussed, and settled, by a local person."

(The weavers' union at Blackburn celebrated its centenary in 1952 by taking all its 10,000 members on a day trip to Blackpool. Meals were provided at a number of restaurants, and later there was dancing at the Tower, *Palace* and Winter Gardens. The *Palace* is no more.)

Clogs and Shawls

THE textile army of Lancashire marched on clogs which, as already related, beat a distinctive tattoo on the flags and setts of the mill towns each morning and evening. How was it that a form of footwear, developed in the Low Countries, became standard wear in north-western England ? Clogs became bound up with Lancashire folk-lore. The Britannia Coconutters of Bacup, who dance every Easter Saturday, manage to wear out their clogs during a 65 mile journey within the borough boundaries.

Weavers from Flanders settled in Lancashire during the 16th century. The immigrants had with them their all-wooden sabots. In course of time—and working to the principle of fitness for purpose—the clog became adapted so that it was suitable for regular wear in the hard, damp environment of Lancashire. The clog acquired a leather top, but retained the wooden sole. The life of the sole was greatly prolonged by the addition of "irons".

Several types of clogs were in use. Pit clogs (or boot clogs) corresponded to boots and came well up the ankles, being secured with natural leather laces. The toes were protected by a heavy steel plate. Such clogs carried no decoration; they were strictly for business, heavy business, such as you would find in a foundry. Ordinary clogs for men fastened with a clasp. Women's clogs, less substantial, were decorated all the way round between the alderwood sole and the welt with brass tacks. A woman's clog had a strap across the instep. The fastener for a child's clog was a button and the clog had more ornamentation, the half-inch broad toepiece of brass being largely a decorative touch. There were even red clogs for a baby. It was the only time that a departure from the traditional black was permitted.

Clogs were not worn in the spinning mill; the iron soles would have knocked up wood on the floors. The operatives often wore their clogs and shawls when going to and from work. Clogs were the customary wear in a weaving shed, where the weaver stood on a flagged floor that was cold and often damp. The clog iron, lifting the wood base clear of the wet floor by a simple one-eighth of an inch, was salvation to the weaver from a health point of view. In the clatter of a shed the little extra noise caused by clogs did not really matter.

Cloggers' shops stood at every street corner. A clogging service was provided by every Co-op. Clogs were, of course, hand-made to the measurements of each customer's feet, and many retail outlets in the Burnley area were supplied with clog blocks by Sam Smalley, a farmer living at Grindleton, who bought up all the alder he could, cut the blocks, and delivered them on a flat cart drawn by a pony. His best customer was the Burnley Co-op. Many of the irons attached to the clogs came from forges at Silsden. The blacksmith, who had provided iron shoes for horses, naturally did this work. Nearly every clogger had a set of bad teeth; he was fond of holding clog tacks in his mouth.

A Colne woman who, as a child, enjoyed going to the clogger said: "Mother didn't like it, though. She had to pay for the repairs!" There was a lame man at the Co-op cloggers. "I remember sitting on a form, in stockinged feet, while he repaired my clogs. Sometimes he'd inspect them and say: 'Oh, there's a big crack in this; I can't mend it.' Then I didn't like to go home to tell mum. When I was 10, my clogs cracked at the toe. It was wet, cold weather. I'd no shoes, and so I couldn't go to school. Mother applied to the town. After a while, an old pair of clogs was sent along to the house. They were a boy's clogs, with a clasp. I wanted a girl's clogs, with a strap."

The thunder of clogs was heard at school as the scholars walked from playground into classroom in tight formations, fearing even to be out of step. A former teacher recalls: "When you got clogs from the clogger they were dull. A boy at school was lined up to have his hands, hair, nails and clogs checked. The clogs that were dull because of newness were overlooked for a week or two, so that the boy had the chance of getting a shine on them. They were given liberal applications of blacking, applied with a stiff brush. Soon they'd be shining like Japanese lacquer. But it took time."

Two crimes with clogs were frowned on by parents. Most boys cracked their clogs on the stone flags to raise sparks. A Burnley man recalled: "I have seen a boy go down a street of 29 houses and at every right-hand step he raised sparks from the ground. By the time he had got to the end, his clog iron was dangling off." Even worse was the tendency of young lads to kick any tin cans they encountered. This frequently led to the shattering of the clog's toepiece.

The clog's day, as the common type of footwear, ended with changing fashions. Young weavers began to wear silk stockings. Many families, having carpets at home, found they were cut to shreds by clog irons. A Burnley man says: "When I was a child, my parents put old woollen stockings round the table legs so that they would not be marked by clogs." Wearing clogs never really died out, but the morning tattoo has not been heard in its old form since the early 1930s.

The shawl, an integral part of the Lancashire mill town image, was made of wool, and generally dark in tone. Every clothier sold shawls. Some of the new owners attached a fringe for decoration. The shawls, large and warm, were capable of covering the head and were frequently kept in place at the chin by a large safety pin. The Lancashire shawl was possibly a development of a smaller shawl used in conjunction with a poke bonnet. The bonnet went out of fashion. The shawl grew in size until it was capable of covering the head.

Traditional clothing for weavers included an apron known as a "brat". It was of constant length, almost reaching to the ground. Men's fashions were not exceptional. Last century a factory operative was reported to be wearing a cloth cap, red neckerchief, check shirt, fustian trousers, waistcoat and clogs.

Life at Home

MOST of the terraced houses we see today had been built by the end of the century. In the period from 1878 to 1918, well over 5,000 new houses were constructed at Accrington, over 300 of them in 1889 alone. The terraced house was the characteristic form. Many an early Lancashire mill town street was no more than eight feet wide, devoid of sewers, and the "night soil" men came stealthily by night to empty the outside privies. In course of time, the quality of building improved. The typical housing scheme was the back-to-back, on a monotonous grid-iron pattern.

Two up, two down, was the rule with regard to many early terraces. Some houses did have a third small space at the ground floor level which became the scullery. The type of house and its furnishings varied with the period and the prosperity or otherwise of the occupying family. A house of pre-1914 vintage was described to me as a "palace" by a Burnley man who told me that the large family was fully employed and could afford to buy their own house, at about £100, and furnish it well. Father was a weaver on six looms, mother had four looms, and two sons were employed at the mill. A young lass had become a tenter. "Father brought in 30 bob a week, mother 19s., the two lads about 18s. each, and a tenter's wage, though smaller, brought the family income up to £5 a week."

The average textile worker was proud of home. "It was spit and polish all the time," said a man at Oswaldtwistle. Each week a flagstone outside the front door was scrubbed down and a rubbing stone applied to colour it. The grim atmospheric conditions led to some women frequently washing the outside of the windows. "It was a famous sight to see the upstairs windows being washed by a woman who would push up the lower frame, sit on the window ledge, with legs dangling inside the bed-

Reveille in a mill town. The Knocker-up, with his pole, to the end of which some wires were attached. A photograph, taken about 1925, shows the windows screened by roller blinds made of paper.

Lancashire weaver, pre-1914. Notice the shawl, which is of shoulder length, and a belt which had a pouch for reed hook and scissors. The mill is illuminated by gas.

A Burnley millscape. The terrace homes of the workers were often in the shadow of their workplace.

Leaving the mill in the days when women wore clogs and shawls. At this pre-1914 period they also wore straw hats.

A cotton mill fire. The fire risk was particularly high in the days of gas illumination.

The morning after a mill fire. Workers survey the blackened stonework and twisted girders.

A mill engine, made at Bolton in 1905, that is now preserved at Darwen.
It provided power for a shed holding 1,224 looms.

A skit on Lancashire poverty. Notice the fireplace, with its flanking oven, side-boiler and high mantelpiece.

Working class district. The coal cart was an unwelcome visitor on washing day. Notice also the donkey, a popular animal for a light cart.

Home of the boss, on the most salubrious side of town. It was the boss's dream to retire to a villa at Southport or St. Annes.

The Christmas goose, and other edibles, displayed with neat precision.
Many a Lancashire meal consisted of bread and jam.

How adventurous people in the pre-1914 period saw the countryside far
from home. Each seat in a charabanc had its own door. Greenwood
Brothers provided the service at Burnley.

room, lower the frame and apply the wash leather vigorously to the glass." The window sills were scrubbed, and the rubbing, or donkey, stone was applied, its tones being cream, white and buff.

With limited accommodation, and large families, an individual had little privacy. A Blackburn man did his school homework with a candle in a little bedroom. Before the 1914-18 war, the furnishings in a poor home were sparse indeed. Much accommodation was rented, and the well-being of the family in hard times depended on the type of landlord involved. A Colne woman recalls: "We paid half-a-crown a week rent. Before I started work, mother found it hard to meet the rent. When she had to get food, the rent missed. Then, next week, she'd pay half-a-crown—plus sixpence off." Many houses, standing near the mills, were owned by the mill company.

A typical terraced house of pre-1914 date had a living kitchen. In the small annexe was a slopstone, the precursor of the sink. A single tap delivered cold water to the slopstone, and underneath was an earthen mug used for washing up and other tasks. Hot water was obtained by putting a pan on the fire or, if a family was lucky, from a side-boiler. Such a fireplace was, at the recollection of a Burnley man, "a great big exhibition of iron, with a fire in the middle and, underneath the fire itself, which was supported on irons, was the ass-oil, or ash hole. The oven occupied one side of the fireplace, with the side-boiler on the other. The set-boiler was a large tank covered with a heavy lid which was lifted by pressure from the thumb." A tap that protruded from the wall on the right-hand side of the fireplace was available for filling the boiler, a task often given to one of the children. "Every now and again, some kid would forget he'd turned on the tap, and he'd go out and play for a minute in the yard. The house was flooded. There was a rare old row!"

The fireplace in such a house was truly a focal point; it demanded to be noticed. "The mantelpiece was a terrific height, getting on for six feet. At either end stood a pottery horse. At least, it was half a horse—a horse sliced down the middle; and the other half stood at the opposite end of the mantelpiece. There might be two pot dogs. In the middle was a clock that never seemed to go right!"

Gas was the servant in most of the houses. A Blackburn man recalls a light fitting with a swan-neck shape, or sometimes two swan-necks, each with a mantle. "Then they introduced 'switch gas', with a pilot light on the fitting. You really were someone in the street if you had this." With gas, a family lived in a half-gloom but did not realise it.

The floors of the oldest houses were flagged. A pegged or "bit" rug occupied a place before the fireside. A Colne woman remembers that her father was fond of making pegged rugs in the winter evenings; "he would have us cutting the material from old clothes into strips. We always had a new rug at the hearth on Christmas morning. The old one was taken to the floor near the slopstone, and we stood on it while washing up. A pegged rug kept your feet warm." When it was decided there was enough money for a carpet to be bought, replacing the pegged rug before the fire, the new carpet was laid on a Saturday morning, then rolled up and stored away on Sunday evening.

Carpets and rugs were rolled up on Friday evening, when the family had a bath, usually one bath, set before the fire, with water replenished from the boiler by way of a lading can. The large, zinc bath was kept on a hook in the back yard. "Mother then washed our hair. We'd sit on a chair and she'd cut our toe nails." Another well-remembered ritual, performed in the living kitchen, was looking through a child's hair for "nits". This was done with a small tooth comb, a white plate being held against the neck. "When a nit fell on the plate, she would crack it with a thumb nail!"

The wood commonly used for furnishings in a living-room was beech. Some poor families made do with a dresser that had a white wood top and consisted of a central cupboard, with drawers on either side. A sideboard of the time had drawers with little brass handles and supported a number of mirrors. The top surface of the sideboard was covered by a "runner" and by fancy mats; a small shelf held cheap ornaments which, none the less, were valued, for they were trinkets brought back by the family or friends from the annual seaside holiday. A draw-leaf table at the centre of the room had a top of pine which was kept scrubbed; the legs were polished. At week-ends, the table was usually covered with a velvet cloth, with "bobbles" round the edge.

Set against a wall in the typical living kitchen was a sofa—not a couch, which has two endpieces. Recalls a Burnley man: "I never knew a sofa that was new. On our sofa, the springs were capable of cutting you into two if you didn't cover them with cushions." A Nelson man remembers the horsehair sofa as something that "pricked little lad's bare legs". At a terraced house in Colne "there was a space under the stairs. At one side was the pantry; at the other the place where we kept the coal. The coalman walked through our living room to deliver coal."

A housewife's sewing machine was often of the type known as "vertical feed", operated by a treadle. One mother is remembered by her daughter as someone who "seemed to spend all her spare time darning, standing directly under the gas light. She could hardly see the dark wool she was using. ... Kind people gave mother clothes; she'd sit up until two or three in the morning, altering them for us kids. She'd no sewing machine, you see. And she had to be out of bed at 6-30 to go to work."

A job performed in the living-room by the children was breaking up a block of salt, using knife and grater. The pieces were placed in a special box that hung on the wall near the fireplace. Here the salt kept dry.

The front room of a terraced house, the "parlour", was used on special occasions, such as for a funeral or when the vicar called. On the window ledge, or a table just inside the window, stood the cherished aspidistra, held in an ornate bowl that stood on a lace "runner". If the room was not "lobbied off", it was simply known as "front place". People using the main door stepped directly into it. A Colne woman says: "I used to clean the front place on Thursday night. I tidied the table, the couch and six chairs, I black-leaded the fireplace. There was a lot of brass to clean: fire irons, ornaments and also a copper kettle."

A piano was a mark of social status. This same woman recalls: "When father left, we had no furniture or anything. The neighbours rallied round. One gave us an old picture, another a mattress that was tatty really. Another handed us a bedhead and foot. While we struggled on to make something of a home, the lady next door used to play a piano. We thought she was really wealthy to have one. She used to let us go in and play the piano. We all sang. That was our entertainment."

Bedrooms were spartan. Says a Burnley man: "If your dad was on six looms, you might have oilcloth on the floor. Most people walked on bare boards that had been put in about 1890 and had shrunk over the years. As you walked, you were conscious of going up and down, and from one board to the next there might be a quarter of an inch crack. What we called 'down' from the bedding collected in the nicks. When mother cleaned up on a Friday, she had to get a skewer or something like that and probe every nick to get out the down."

At Colne it was related: "Someone gave us a bed. I'd always wanted a bed that was black, with brass knobs. This bed had been painted green. We had a straw mattress given. It had a lot of fleas. I helped my mother to bray camphor balls, and we sprinkled them in the mattress. Mother spent her holidays doing special jobs about the house. One year, I remember, she white-washed the bedroom walls. There was wallpaper on them when we went there. We hadn't enough money to redecorate properly."

The old 'uns talked of the days when a poor family slept five to a bed, arranged tops and tails, the coverings including a piece of brown paper that crinkled all night. The bed frames were of iron, painted black, and the uprights held little brass knobs. The Burnley man remembers flock beds. When mother decided they must be "turned over" it was a job to "tow thi guts out". Patchwork quilts were popular because they could be made at home, out of odds and ends of material from clothing.

In the era of privy/middens, which were in outbuildings, summertime was characterised by the vast number of houseflies that buzzed around the houses. Long, sticky "fly papers" adorned the gas-brackets indoors. The early privy, which was also known as "closet" or "petty", was simply a large container that was periodically emptied by the "night soil men". Later came the tippler; when this filled with liquid it tipped over and the contents descended direct into the sewer.

The ash pit was emptied by men who raked it out on to the back street and loaded it into a cart for transportation to the tip. As the men cleared the street, a small army of women appeared with brushes and pails and devoted themselves to "swilling". Until the 1920s the refuse was taken away by horse and cart; then petrol-driven lorries were being introduced. In 1928, the borough of Blackburn was divided into three districts, each with a two-ton motor, but additionally a horse and four-wheeled cart were employed on the shorter hauls and occasionally an extra horse and cart were brought in to relieve congestion in any one district.

Washday at a terraced home almost attained the status of a religious ceremony. Its success was judged on the weariness of the housewife at the end of the day. If she was not prostrate with exhaustion, she had not done the job well! "It was a real upset day," a Colne woman recalls. "And there was ironing to do at night."

An early start was vital. The water was boiled in a zinc, three-legged boiler. "You got up in the morning, fixed on the gas pipe, ignited it and got on with other tasks while the water was heating. Then you got out the wash-tub, which in the old days was a proper cooper's job, like a beer barrel, perfectly made, absolutely watertight. Then it was a case of washing all day. Clothes in the tub were stirred by a posser or, earlier, by a dolly, which was a three-legged device with a vertical shaft and a handle for twirling. You sweated all day with the dolly—up and down and round; lift and turn, lift and turn—and you added a bit of dolly blue to the water to whiten the clothes."

The mangle used for abstracting the water was monstrous, "with a big iron wheel on one side, yet the average housewife—a half-starved little woman—turned it unrelentingly." In the course of time, the wooden rollers became worn and splintered. The middle section became so worn you could put your fist between the rollers. "Then you used either end of the roller. If you were not careful the clothes slipped off into the greasy cogs!"

The first batch of clothes, the most valuable, were hung in the yard. "This was the stuff you couldn't afford to have pinched—though I must say thefts were few." The remaining clothes were strung from lines extending across the back street. Nearly every housewife washed on Monday. The back streets had hundreds of items of clothes hanging from end to end. "On a March day, when the clothes were blowing, they were quite a pretty sight."

The villain on washday was the coalman, with his horse and cart. "If he decided to come up the back street, you'd soon have 20 or 30 housewives threatening him. If there was just the odd line of clothes—as, for evample, if someone found it necessary to wash on a Tuesday—the wife and children would appear with props, hoist up the lines, throw the clothes over them and let the coalman go through. That was exceptional. It was certain death for a coalman or dustman to go up a back street on washing day."

Traditional Food

OFTEN, in the lean days, there was bread, butter and jam on the menu, day in and day out. A weaver's daughter said: "Many a time, if it was getting near pay day and mother had only one warp in, there'd be a slice of bread each for us—nothing for her. I remember her cutting a single piece of bread and handing out the pieces with the words: 'Go to your auntie, and ask her to put some margarine on it.' It was always like that just before pay day."

Most of the traditional delicacies of the past are available today.

Black Pudding. Long before the Industrial Revolution, the pig figured largely in the Lancashireman's diet. Pork products were popular in the mill towns. Black puddings have been prepared in Bury on a commercial basis since at least 1818.

When a pig was slain, its blood was collected in a bucket and stirred—traditionally with the arm up to the elbow—until it coagulated and darkened. To it were added groats and pieces of fat about the size of dice. Herbs gave added flavouring. Black puddings were made using skins from pig intestines: they first resembled fat sausages, but by the time the ends had been drawn together and tied, the general appearance was spherical.

A black pudding stall at an old time market was simply a trestle table, with a boiler standing on the ground at one end. The gas supply came via underground pipe, the end of which was exposed when the stallholder removed a selected sett. The trestle held salt, pepper and vinegar.

If a family purchased some boiled puddings for later consumption, these would be sliced, then fried in fat.

Tripe. A market stall supplied a pennyworth of tripe bits, to which salt and vinegar were added. The tripe was served on a plate, with a piece of bread and butter added.

Tripe had the merit of being a cheap dish and was nourishing. Easily digested, it was reputed to "clean the stomach". A thin form of tripe came from sheep. "Black tripe", from a cow's belly, resembled a dish-clart (cloth). When displayed for sale, efforts were made to impart attractiveness by setting it on a white marble slab with other varieties of tripe, the whole display being adorned with tomatoes and lettuce.

Elder. The udder of a cow, elder was yellow-tinged, though with a general greyish-brown hue. Elder had an excellent flavour. It was always sliced thin and traditionally, was eaten with salt, vinegar, pepper and brown bread and butter.

Pigs' Trotters. These have had a special association with Bolton, the local football team being known as "Trotters". The dish consists of the edible parts of a pig's foot, boiled at the tripe works, the cleaves being torn away with the use of a special hook. When boiled, it resembled a mass of transparent jelly, slightly yellow in hue. It was eaten with salt. Cow heel, similar to pig's trotter, came, of course, from the cow.

Meat and Potato Pie. A staple food in many working class homes, the meat was usually beef. Corner shops had such pies for sale to textile operatives at dinnertime. The Lancashire Hot Pot was traditionally of mutton chops, or bones and scraps left over from the Sunday meat dish, covered with thin, sliced potatoes. It was not mash. The sliced potatoes remained flat and distinctive. A few vegetables, such as peas, lentils and sliced carrots, might be added.

Polony. Akin to sausage meat, this was contained in red skin. It was, conveniently, supplied in a cooked state.

Hot Peas. Lancashire towns once had their "pay 'oils", or pea holes, known primly as Hot Pea Saloons. Two or three cauldrons were to be seen, and in them were various types of pea, which were sold in small white basins, about 3 inches deep. Salt and vinegar were available. Children usually took quick "swigs" from the vinegar bottle if no one was looking! A helping of peas cost a halfpenny; one ate the peas and then drank off the liquid. Alternatives to the main dish of green peas were "greys" and "pigeon peas". The latter actually rattled in the mouth. A penny meat pie was available. If gravy was added, the customer watched the retailer make a hole in the top of the pie with his thumb to admit the gravy!

Cakes. Bury was famous for its simnel cake, which was originally of religious significance. So were Eccles cakes, at first sold at fairs or wakes. A third distinctive Lancashire delicacy was the Chorley cake.

Before the 1914-18 war, as indicated, many poor families breakfasted on bread and butter. Marmalade was somewhat cheaper to buy than jam and was contained in a large pot jar. When empty, this pot was partly filled with hot water, which was then swilled round by the children, who drank a faintly flavoured liquid called "sipings". Rice puddings were a general standby throughout the year. Plum duff, served in winter, was known as "stick-in-the-ribs".

Tuesdays and Fridays were "fish days". Major Tattersall — Major was his Christian name, not a military title—toured parts of Burnley with a flat cart divided into sections. Plaice was the choice of those with money to spare, but the poorer families selected "garnets", or "gurnards"—large, ugly fish notable for their incredible number of bones. If, during the meal, someone spluttered as a bone stuck in his throat, a piece of dry bread was gulped on the theory that "if yon bone won't come up, it'll go down!"

Tinned salmon was kept until week-end, and the arrival of "comp'ny" for tea. For the family, salmon was mixed with bread crumbs, forming a paste, and liquid margarine was poured on to it.

What happened when the larder was bare? A Colne woman

recalls: "When the general strike was on, we'd no food. A man came from the Labour Party. He knocked at the door and said: 'Nah then, Mary Anne, I've brought you these.' There was flour, some barm (yeast), jam, margarine and tea. Mother set to and soon had the oven going. She baked some bread. It was lovely bread."

Poverty Knock

IN a series of sermons given in 1904 and 1905, the Rev. R. M. Julian, minister of Ebenezer Baptist Church at Burnley, referred to "blots on our town"—drunkenness, crime, and an exceptionally high infant mortality rate. These, he said, were symptoms of deeper-rooted evils. "There are warrens within 10 minutes walk of this chapel that are unfit in every way for human habitation. They are kept in wretched repair ... The only exit is a narrow entry, and if tonight the lamp was turned over in a drunken quarrel, many men, women and children would be roasted alive because there are no means of escape."

Indeed, over 1,000 people lived in one-roomed homes in Burnley at the time when the minister spoke. He mentioned the lamentable absence of hygiene, especially where mothers at work had to leave their infants with other women during the day. Mr. Julian also noted that many expectant mothers had to work in the mills right up to the time of delivery; it was no wonder that the infant mortality was high.

There was general poverty in the mill towns late last century; later, conditions improved a little but the workers faced the periodical onset of austerity when they were on short time or actually out of work. In 1926, the time of the general strike, soup kitchens were a common sight, and a man attending one of them observed: "It's nobbut t'poor as helps t'poor." Kindly people made broth and soup, filling the basins produced by those in need; they cared especially for the children. Meat came from a friendly butcher who could get cheap offal. Philanthropists distributed cast-off clothes, also clogs. In the lean times, the pawnbrokers throve. The "moonlight flit" was a common way out of a dilemma when a family could no longer afford the rent.

A Colne woman, recalling the late 1920s, mentioned being sent into the centre of town late on Saturday night to visit a fish shop whose owner, wishing to clear his stock, would shout: "Any fish you like for a tanner." The same woman declares that "we did not always have enough to eat. Mam sometimes used up all the food, or she may just have enough bread to cut us three children a thick slice each at dinnertime. Then she'd say to us: 'Go to your grandma, and ask her to put you some marg. on it. I'll pay her back when I get my wage after work tonight'."

The aunt of a Burnley man who did not earn £1 a week in her long working life—in a full week, when she was not "coving" she drew 19s.—told me his father was on 26s. a week, "and if he'd had a row with the boss there wasn't a week. I've had many a tin of beans for supper. It was called pork and beans in those days. There was a piece of pork about half the size of your thumb in it. Once, mother said: 'Put a can of beans on that fire, love.' I didn't realise she meant 'Put it in a pan!' I dropped it straight on the fire, on the hot coals. You can guess what happened. There was an almighty bang; the tin flew off. It was as clean as if you'd washed it out with soap and water and dried it with a tea towel." Another Burnley man might have gone to the grammar school if funds allowed. Mother said: "Ay, lad, th'heart's willing, but purse isn't."

When people were really hard up, and it was a choice of food or fire, it was a case of keeping the fire going, even to the extent of breaking up furniture as fuel. The proverb was: "Last penny goes on fire." In the meanest of homes, meals were always "scratch" and the table never seemed to be cleared. "They couldn't afford cow's milk as a rule. Nestle's milk was the commonest kind. Bread and jam were the staples. In the most poverty-stricken homes, it was mainly bread."

The education authority provided food, of a sort, but not on the school premises. Recalls a native of Burnley: "Two lads, brothers, were literally starving. We'd lots of thin lads in our class of 60. These two lads were so thin they got free meals. At a minute to noon, every day, they turned out, went to the headmaster's desk, received a ticket each, and walked a mile and a half down into town, in summer heat or winter snow, without coats. They went to a wooden hut where one or two women supervised two cauldrons. These lads, standing in the open, were each given a bowl and a chunk of bread. The bowl was first filled with a brown stew from one cauldron, and when this was drunk they got a ladle full of white stuff from the second cauldron. They cleaned bowls out with pieces of bread and handed them back to the women. The lads then walked back to school."

Here is a story from Colne, c. 1929: "My sister taught me how to weave. I went on two looms. The business failed. We started to 'weave up'. Then we were on the dole." This woman was one of three sisters. "At the Labour Exchange I was asked if I was friendly with the other two. We were entitled to 3s. a week each; but only one need turn up to collect it. I went next Friday and got 9s. Many a time it was all we as a family had to live on. We used to get stuff from the shop on tick."

She added: "The Catholic nuns at Colne were good to us. They had a little private school and quite a few pupils from well-to-do homes. Parents who were nicely off gave clothes to the nuns, who handed them out to needy children. Sometimes I went home with stockings or gloves."

The hardships of the early 1930s were the worst in living memory. A weaver who had money and became a butcher turned up at one mill with carcasses of mutton. He set up shop in a corner of the warehouse, selling the mutton cheaply. The dole queues were long. A Nelson man, thinking of his childhood, recalls the day his mother came home with 4 oz. of butter she had bought at the Co-op. "It was a winter's day. She put the butter in a dish and asked me to hold it by the fire to soften it. The pat of butter slipped into the flames. I can see it in my mind's eye all these years afterwards: the butter went black and melted. Mum clattered me for 20 minutes. Really thumped me. I thought it was unjust. Now I know that the situation at home was desperate."

A bleacher, of Bolton, says that during the bad times it was customary for textile concerns to accept various commodities from abroad in lieu of money. An example was tea, from Ceylon. "They couldn't pay for their goods. The Manchester merchants accepted payment in kind. We, because of our federation rules, couldn't accept barter. We used to buy a lot of stuff, though. I remember there was a wonderful orange tea at a shilling a pound. The tea was all done up in foil."

The pawnshop was the only bridge a poor family had between the wages of Friday and the poverty of the rest of the week. A wife would get her husband's suit out of pawn on Friday night, so that he would have something good to wear at the week-end, and the suit went back into pawn until the following Friday. A man who wore a collar and tie at week-ends had a white muffler round his neck during the week. A Bolton spinner says: "It was a matter of pride to be well-dressed at week-ends. A man always had money for a packet of cigarettes, a pint of beer and to let him watch Bolton Wanderers play football on a Saturday afternoon."

Families attempting to buy their own houses managed to pay off the interest. The capital figure did not change for years on end.

Families lived in dread of the workhouse. A Blackburn man who regularly visited a workhouse, when apprenticed to an electrician, to attend to the fittings, recalls the many tramps. "Every night, they came into the casual wards. They had left their meagre possessions tucked in cracks and crannies in the big wall at the approach to the gate. A man arriving at Blackburn might have come from the workhouse at Chorley or Bolton, walking through the villages, scrounging what he could.

"On admission to the workhouse, he'd have a bath and his clothes would be fumigated—though this had happened recently at the previous workhouse. Tramps were the cleanest people in Lancashire! He'd be given a piece of bread and cheese and a big mug of tea, and he went to bed. On the following day, he had some task to do—chopping firewood, or something like that. During the morning, he'd have a piece of bread and marg., and later he got a decent dinner, then a jam tea. He was off the following morning, picking up his meagre possessions from the wall and heading for the next workhouse, maybe Preston."

Visiting a relative at a workhouse was humiliating to many. A permit was needed. A Burnley visit is remembered: "You presented yourself at the workhouse gates, and were ushered into a little office. When you were summoned, you went into a big hall, where there were chairs and tables. You found your relative and handed over some of life's little basics—butter, sugar, tea, rice, lard, a bit o' bacon, and such like. Once you'd gone, these provisions were added to the general stock of goods at the institution."

In hard times, people were forced to stay at or near home. Says a Nelson man: "I remember a local house because the area between the picture rail and the ceiling was covered with paintings of the Lancashire countryside. Yes, they had been painted on the top part of the wall. Some poor chap was remembering the old days, when he was mobile!"

Speech and Song

I ASKED an elderly man in Accrington about the expression "All a-flunters", to be told it meant "in a reight pickle". When I queried this he answered, a little wearily: "All mucked up". From which you will gather that the old speech of Lancashire is not dead. It is often more expressive than standard English. Many books have been written about Lancashire dialect. My concern is with a few special words and phrases to be heard in the mill towns.

Each mill town has its accent. The Oldham accent was explained to me as "reight in th'mouth, which flops about." That of Rochdale, a few miles away, and also of Burnley, was described as "a rounded sort of speech; all vowel sounds, pushed out at mouth top". Wigan folk, I was told, appear to chew their words.

Peter Wright, in *Lancashire Dialect,* quotes: "E lives back-beams to us" (behind us); "Ah'm stopped fer bobbins" (out of work); or sadly, "Ah've woven mi piece" (I'm almost at the end of my life).

A dialect glossary explains some of the regularly used words: *aboon* for above; *addle some brass* for earning some money; *brat* for an apron; *flit* for remove house; *fratch* signifying to argue. If you are asked to *howd on* you must pause.

A common expression I heard is "Na think on ..." meaning "please remember". Years ago, one heard "I'll leather thee" or "I'll belt thee", meaning to thrash a youngster (the domestic "strap", which usually hung from a hook at the fireside, may have started out life as belting in a local mill). An example of the type of speech that could be heard in the mill towns was: "Hoo were fair clammed cos hoo'd gin all we had to eyt to childer." This can be translated as: "She was starved because she had given all the food she possessed to the children."

An example of how an expression, derived from a specialist occupation, could change in course of time is provided by: "Beaten up some Sampson", which is now rarely heard. In poverty-stricken days, a meal could be provided by beating up a raw egg in a basin and adding some sweetening and milk; thus a mother could give an equal share of the egg to each of several children. The words used by the mother were: "Eyt it oop, and then thou'll be strong, same as Sampson." In course of time, the expression became, simply "Sampson".

Many words preserved in Lancashire dialect are of Anglo-Saxon origin; they include the *brat* (derived from bratt, meaning a cloak); *fain* for glad (from the word faegen); *een* (eye), *shoon* (shoes), *clom* (climb). Lancashire speyks reflect the spontaneous, warm humour of the towns, and they include: "If thou'd any more mouth thou'd hev no face to wash."

Allen Clarke recorded: "There's nowt lost by axin" (you'll lose nothing if you ask); "theau't eitin' nowt" (your appetite is poor); "a still tongue allus shows a wise yead" (the wise say little), and "there's nowt mooar witchin' i' th'world nor a widow" (a widow is most beguiling).

The vocal side of mill town life had an enormous range—from the chapel choir, rendering *The Messiah* just before Christmas, to pub-singing. Many hymns bear the names of Lancashire towns, even streets. The most famous, *Rimington*—named after a village lying near Pendle Hill — was composed by Francis Duckworth, whose family had moved to Colne, where he became a successful grocer and also organist at the Albert Road chapel. *Rimington*, published in 1904, was sung for the first time at the Colne Whitsuntide processions, to the hymn with which it has been most strongly associated: "Jesus shall reign where'er the sun". The tune came in the heyday of religious gatherings, and 20,000 people sang it at Nelson. It became a special favourite with bandsmen, and featured in some early broadcasts. The appeal of the hymn to missionary organisations ensures its world-wide popularity. A Rev. Hartley composed a song called "Barrowford, all on one side", to be sung to the tune *Bonny Colne*.

Many of the songs rendered in public houses had a countryside origin, and there were parodies on music hall songs. Lancashire had a strong, spontaneous tradition for making up words to much-loved tunes, or even for redeveloping tunes, such as this rip-off of a terrible music hall song:

> *Call round any old time,*
> *Mak thissen at home,*
> *Put thi feet on the mantel-shelf,*
> *Sit by the fire and help thiself.*

I don't care if your pals
Have left thi all alone:
Rich or poor, knock on the door,
Make thiself at home.

Old Lancashire songs — and many new pieces — have been recorded by groups of folk-singers. The poems of the 19th century giants, such as Waugh, continue to flavour our thinking about Lancashire. William Barron well demonstrated the puckish Lancashire humour, delivered low-key, with repressed sentimentality.

Cradle to Grave

Even as late as the 1930s, there was a stigma attached to any girl who had a child out of wedlock. Or as a Blackburn man says: "If a girl *had* to be married, it was looked on as something terrible. Pre-marital sex was usually avoided, and I'm not sure whether it was a question of morality—or fear." Comparatively few males were married before the age of 24, with the girl slightly younger. With the birth of a child, in the days before maternity hospitals were commonplace, there was a doctor or an experienced amateur midwife living nearby; the birth was invariably in one of the bedrooms.

Child mortality was high by modern standards. It was assumed that someone in a large family would die from an infection like scarlet fever. Says a Burnley woman: "If a small boy died from diphtheria, everyone was sorry, but no one was surprised. It was an act of God; it was accepted." In the case of an epidemic, the sufferers were conveyed to an isolation hospital, on the outskirts of town, by special van. Measles were borne with various degrees of cheerfulness at home. A Colne weaver says: "If we had measles, mother couldn't stay off work to look after us. We needed the money she brought in. She had just to leave us and go to the mill."

Came the time for courtship. A Blackburn man recalls of the 1930s: "We used to go into the country a lot. We went for miles. I was 20 when I met my wife, and we got engaged after about a year, saving up like mad for the ring during that first year. Walking was the cheapest form of courtship; one frosty night we sat down for so long we were too stiff and cold to move!"

A Colne girl met her boy—she "got off" with him—during a week-end visit to one of the "monkey walks", stopping to talk, then arranging to walk together, with perhaps a visit to a local fish and chip shop, or to the man who sold pies and peas. "If they found they liked one another, it would continue from there. Otherwise it just fizzled out." There were three Monkey Walks at Burnley. "One went to the Tram Shed along the Prairie, and no one walked any further," says a retired weaver. "Some walked all evening. The police moved in when anyone stopped in a doorway. But there was no real trouble—not like there is today."

How often a girl was allowed by her mother to go courting depended on whether or not mother was working. Most girls had to help out in the home during the evening. The late Alice Foley, who entered a Bolton mill full-time in 1905, recorded that the monotonous drudgery of machine-tending was occasionally broken by tradtional "footings", when a workmate announced her approaching marriage. "This usually took the form of a mock procession down the broad-alley, the bride-to-be being draped in a curtain or white sheet, followed by a squealing cluster of well-wishers, the elder ones offering ribald jokes, the younger girls giggling to hide their embarrassment." Later, the workers were regaled with "pop, pies and Eccles cakes in a community mood of hearty fellowship".

It was known for a Lancashire couple to be married during the dinner break; the happy couple returned to the looms after that brief interval and continued to weave until the mill closed at 5-30.

Courtship was devoted to acquiring enough money to start off a home. A couple was fortunate if there was space at home for them to have one or more of the rooms. The wedding reception was invariably held at the parents' home.

Everyone had a weekly reminder of impending death, for it was the custom for families to dress in their best clothes on a Sunday afternoon and walk round the local cemetery. This was not a morbid experience. Friends were encountered, and there was quite cordial talk about the dear departed. During life, a person saved hard so that there might be a funeral of a type to indicate respectability. The real fear in old Lancashire was of being "buried by the parish".

Piety was shown when announcing a death in the local newspaper. Quotations included: "Fought hard, but lost" or "We

63

cannot, Lord, thy purpose see, but all is well that's done by thee." Every newspaper has a book of such quotations, numbered for easy reference, and they were used generously. Before the coffin lid was screwed down, relatives and friends were invited to view the corpse. A man whose first job was that of a milkboy, aged 15, recalls with merriment how, when he first delivered milk to one house, a woman asked him if he wanted to see her father. He said: "All right." She took him into the house, and there was dad, lying in his coffin!

Allen Clarke described a cab horse used for funerals as a "lean, dismal horse that looked as if it had been fed on grave-wreaths and stalled in cemeteries all its life." Even working class folk hired horse-drawn hearses and cabs (to be superseded in modern times by motor hearses that, similarly, were shining black). A Colne woman whose family had little money recalls that, when a brother died, a hearse and single cab were hired for the immediate relatives. "Mother said to the others that if they wanted to attend the funeral they must provide their own transport. So they got together, and arranged for two more cabs. Afterwards we returned to the house. Mother had cooked some meat and made some cakes. We ate them. That was that."

Matters of the Mind

THE factory came first in the list of local institutions, school being the place to tolerate until one might leave and start work. Religion was a powerful influence in local affairs, a balm to a host of working people and, quite often, salve for the social conscience of the manufacturers. Many were nonconformists. They gave their time and money liberally—and prominently—to the causes.

Education

Lancashire cotton was competitive when there was a handy reservoir of inexpensive juvenile labour. By the Education Act of 1870, the attendance of children between the ages of five and 13 was made compulsory, but children were exempt at 10 if they wished to become half-timers at the mill. The system and its conditions were improved by successive Acts. With the spread of education, consideration was shown towards health and welfare. At Burnley, eyesight and teeth were regularly examined. A school clog fund was established in 1905.

The oldest among us remember when education was based, firmly, on acquiring knowledge of the Three Rs, and when even the time taken to mark the register was not wasted. Ten unfamiliar words were written on the blackboard and the children must learn them before the last name was called out. For most children, education ended when they left day school. Others benefited from the night schools and institutes of further education.

A Bolton man recalls: "Father worked his way up from being a half-timer; he started work at the mill at the age of 10½ years, and became a full-time employee when he was 13. Yet by going to school in the evening he acquired an education equal to the best at university. He had first-class honours in scripture and science; he studied mathematics and English; he taught himself shorthand, and then improved on Pitman's system because he found it was not quite good enough for his kind of work. Only a few people went from the ordinary bottom levels of education right through to the top."

A Burnley man remembers dashing home from the mill at 5-30; he would wash, change, have a meal and dash off to an evening class. "I went five nights a week and on Saturday afternoons. This was part of my training as a cabinet-maker. In 1916 I was indentured and worked 53 hours for 6s. a week. I still went to night school from 7 to 9 p.m. And remember, in those days you had to be at work at 6 a.m."

At Nelson, many organisations arranged activities of an educational nature. There were Assembly Rooms above the Co-op shops, and some of the cultural activities here were Co-op inspired. A grateful supporter said: "In the centre of town stood the Co-op Hall, which in winter offered celebrity lantern lectures. In the 1930s, I saw people like Eric Shipton and Frank Smythe. It was threepence to go in and listen to them." One notable lecturer at Burnley in about 1932 was Ponting, who went to the Antarctic with Scott.

Religion

In 1928, the Sunday Schools of Accrington were congratulated on the part they played in keeping down crime. It was not a primary objective, but many were indeed grateful for the wholesome life that was offered by two Sunday services, two sessions of Sunday School, and a host of weekday activities. "It was no penance to attend Sunday School in those days; children actually looked forward to it," I was told at Blackburn. "There was much more social activity connected with the chapels. The Salvation Army was, and is, a great force for good."

At Whitsuntide, a form of stock-taking was provided by the annual Walks. Walter Bennett has recorded that at Nelson, one of the smaller towns, in 1901, nine Sunday Schools produced 4,500 scholars. The figures in 1923 were 21 and 6,000. By the early 1930s, a decline was experienced, and in 1931 a total of 21 schools yielded 3,400 scholars. The Walks were, and are, a characteristic feature of springtime in the mill towns. "If you were very privileged, you rode on the wagon," says a Nelson man. "If you were not, you walked. The processions set off from the different churches, each with its tall banners, and then you'd get this sudden, dramatic convergence on the centre of town. The traditional offering to the children afterwards consisted of buns and coffee."

At Blackburn, Mrs. Lewis had her Teetotal Mission. She intercepted wage-earners as they went home, before they had the chance to visit public houses with their pay packets. A local man remembered the mission premises: "Round the room were the classical texts, such as 'Lips that tough liquor shall never touch mine.' Parodies on popular hymns were sung. I remember the words *Cwm Rhonda* included: 'Save the drunkard, save the drunked, save him now and ever more.' The whole emphasis at this mission was to get people to sign the pledge."

Religious and political organisations had their highly vocal representatives in Blackburn market place on Sunday evenings. A man who tried most of them eventually found solace and a challenge at the Queen's Hall Methodist Mission. Though it held 1,760 people, many could not get a seat. Those were the days when there were few alternative forms of diversion. He remembers a preacher called Noel L. Hutchcroft, who had a rich baritone voice and had at heart the social implications of the Christian message. He was thus a typical "mission man". In the depression years he ran a soup kitchen for the poorer people of Blackburn. "He would tour the streets, a muffler across his face, and press pennies into the hands of the needy, telling them of the mission and the soup and bread they could get there. He ran celebrity concerts for the unemployed."

The Blackburn man remembered the band with which he set out on Friday evening. It was a means of inviting people to attend the Sunday evening service. "I used to go to a men's class on a

Thursday with about 80 men. It was a terrific class, though when I think about it now I do not think the theology of the hymns was very good. They had good tunes—and the members liked bawling their heads off!"

Politics

At Nelson, the Conservative and Liberal parties dominated the scene until 1890, when two Labour candidates were first returned to the borough council. Nelson went far-left politically. The town held a large branch of the Communist Party in the early 1920s, and when Richard Winterbottom, Mayor of Nelson from 1929 to 1931, would not allow the national anthem to be played at any events he attended, the town was given the name "Little Moscow".

A Burnley man remembers when Dan Irving, the first local Socialist of significance, supported the Tories and was stated to have "gone ower". It happened at the second of two meetings attended by Lord Derby. "My dad was standing on a stool at the back of the Mechanics' Hall. He called out something, and he got thrown down the 13 steps outside. He hit every one of those steps and lost his new hat. He'd paid 6s. 9d. for the hat that very morning!"

The manufacturers tended to be either Tory or Liberal. An increasing number of workers joined the Labour Party at a time when its leaders, both nationally and locally, were practising Christians. Says a Nelson man: "The Labour Party I remember as a child was there for one purpose: to try and improve the conditions of the people who had to work for a living."

I heard that in the past, textile workers seemed to be more Tory-minded than Labour-minded. A peculiar situation arose between union members in Blackburn. Some decided they did not want any money to go to the Labour Party, so they formed their own union, called the Protection Society, nick-named the Tory Club. The Blackburn and district Weavers', Winders' and Warpers' Association became known as the Labour Club. Much later, they merged.

Out and About

THE millfolk lacked the mobility that is taken for granted today. At Easter and times of national celebration, many hundreds of them walked from the cotton towns to the summit plateau of Pendle. Pedestrians visited Paythorne, by the Ribble, each November, on the day declared to be Salmon Sunday. They hoped to see some fish on the move.

Cycling. The cycle provided many urban-dwellers with a cheap form of transport to selected rural beauty spots, often at considerable distances. A former cyclist recalls: "The ordinary people could scarcely afford to use the buses and trains, and the tram routes were rather limited. In my own case, the cycle meant I could get up to Ribblehead and Dent and be back home at night. Sixty miles a day was chicken feed. Sunday was the great cycling day because, remember, we were working in the mill till mid-day on Saturday."

At Colne, it is recalled: "My brother bought a bike for a pound —and he started cycling regularly. Then he decided to buy a tandem, so he could take me out. One tandem that suited us cost £16 second-hand. Mother wondered how to pay for it. An auntie who'd married a tackler and was quite well off lent us the money. Then grandfather died. He'd been poorly for quite a while. Grannie had enough on insurance to bury him properly. Mother's insurance money paid off the loan. Grandfather gave us that tandem, you might say."

The Cyclists' Touring Club had many adherents. Hundreds converged on villages like Bolton-by-Bowland for special meets. The C.T.C. sign, signifying that meals were available to cyclists, was to be seen on farms and cottages over a wide area. At Nelson, a cycling club for older people became known as *The Autumn Tints*. A man called Shackleton thought nothing of setting off on his bike to cover 30 miles when he was well into his 70s.

The Trams. Electric traction on the tramways of Lancashire appeared towards the end of the 19th century. Bolton's first electric tramcar was operating in 1899, and within four years the enterprising transport department had begun to experiment with a motor bus service, but not until 1923 did the motor bus begin its regular rounds.

"The trams offered fabulous journeys for coppers," I heard at Bolton. "For example, from here you could go to Horwich, Rochdale, then Stockport, with periodical changes of vehicle but in a continuous line. The track was of the same gauge." At Burnley, single-deck trams were necessary for the negotiation of a tunnel under the canal — tunnels known as "gimlet 'oils". Double-deckers were more typical of Lancashire vehicles.

Motor Vehicles. Early vehicles, named charabancs, gave hundreds of people their first long excursions. "You climbed into a sort of toast-rack thing, with a door for every seat, and did a variety of tours. One of them was the Great North Round." In the days of solid tyres, a Burnley double-decker bus adventurously travelled with sightseers to York.

Deacons, of Belmont, were almost certainly the first company to take cloth from a Lancashire works—they were bleachers and dyers—to Manchester by steam lorry; the year was 1899. The distance between Belmont and the company's offices in the city was 18 miles, and the lorry, with a four-ton load, made the trip comfortably in under four hours.

The Railway. Lancashire was densely patterned with railways. The chief company was the *Lancashire and Yorkshire*, with its main offices in Horwich and Manchester and many huge warehouses for the storage of cotton at stations across the county. From here, the raw cotton was distributed by horse and cart.

The locomotives of the company were black, and the carriages were famous for their horsehair seats. A Bolton man told me: "When I was very small, and wearing short trousers, those cushions were irritating; they prickled the backs of my legs." Gas-type illumination is just remembered. A railwayman ran along the roof of a carriage with a torch, lifting lids and igniting the gas jet below. Corridor coaches were not general, for Lancashire journeys tended to be short. It was for this reason that the company used tank engines. "Large tenders were not needed."

A man started work for the *L & Y* in 1921 at 24s. a week; he was 15 years old. Long retired, he recollects that "the safety valves on a locomotive were of Ramsbottom type, and we had to scour them with powder. The loco itself was washed down with soft soap and water."

As railways began to lose the battle against road transport, some fabulous halfpenny-a-mile journeys were being offered.

The Horse Days. Horses drew the wagonettes of the wealthy, the big wagons of industry, a variety of carts used by traders—including the ubiquitous coal merchant—and were put in the shafts of scores of cabs that were available, night and day, for special journeys.

The horses themselves were characters. Recalls a Bolton man: "A carter would take an outfit to Manchester in the morning with a load of cloth, and pick up goods for the return journey. The horses knew, on the return trip, at which pubs they should stop. They usually completed the last part of the journey without help from the carter. The man was either drunk or asleep. I have seen horses bring a big wagon right into a mill yard."

A carter working out of Burnley stopped the laden cart at the top of the hill in Manchester Road and went across the road to an inn. The landlady commented on the kindness of a small boy, who was seen to be feeding the horse. The carter looked and swore. The lad was using his "bait", or mid-day meal, which the carter had left under the cart seat.

Two horses could pull a cart on reasonably flat ground, and other horses were readily available at stables for a short haul up any notorious incline, such as from a mill in the valley to a main road. A man who rented part of a mill at Burnley in the period just before the 1914-18 war notes that it would take four hours for a horse-hauled cart to reach Manchester. The carters set off at about 6 a.m., arrived in the city by mid-morning. They unloaded and made their way back, collecting yarn from the spinning mills. Cloth was delivered to Manchester warehouses from the Burnley area on Tuesdays and Fridays.

Some horses were ill-treated. A common offence was working a horse with a sore under its collar. The sore was, naturally, covered up, not apparent to passers-by. A Burnley man observes: "The poor cab horse could be called out at any time of day or night. In recent times, I met a man who admitted that his firm would work a horse uphill and downhill, all day long. and bed it down for the night as late as 10 p.m., only to rouse it again in the early hours, when an emergency arose." Horses could be ill-treated to such a pitch they would "stall", or become prostrate, unable to rise from where they had slumped on the ground.

Life in the Streets

The wind, the wind, the wind blows high
The rain comes scattering from the sky;
She is handsome, she is pretty,
She is a girl of London city.

So chanted the small girls as they skipped in the back streets on spring and summer evenings. Other favourite songs were "In and out the window", "There was a jolly miller", "Here comes the duke a-riding" and—to accompany a game—"Here comes one lame soldier out of work". When the children sang "Green grow the leaves on the oak tree", were they perpetuating the spirit of pre-industrial Lancashire?

A man who remembers the pre-1914 period says: "We played the children's knur and spell, which we called 'buck and stick'. The stick was quite often an old picking stick from the mill; it was an ash stick, very hard. You tipped the buck, which flew into the air, and then you ran. We played marbles with glass balls taken from pop bottles. We had a game called 'Tin in t'Ring', in which someone would throw the tin and call out another's name. All but that person ran off. The one whose name was called had to collect the tin."

Small girls played "chopping stones", or "chops", which was a corruption of shops, using handfuls of powder made from such objects as red brick, broken pottery and bottles. The blue bottle that had held poison was greatly prized. The iron hoop appeared as the days lengthened in early spring. As an alternative to metal hoops, made by the blacksmith, you might have a wooden hoop and stick, the type seen on sentimental Victorian pictures. Children's wheelbarrows were invariably painted red inside, yellow outside.

In the world of factory, chimney and massed houses there was a strange survival of the old days: the maypole, produced on the first day of May. A Burnley man recalls: "It was a broom handle with two wooden hoops fixed on the top. The hoops were interlaced, decorated with specially frilled paper of various colours. A bell hung from the hoops, and at the top was the semblance of a crown. Ribbons extended from the top of the broomstick. A small group of girls, usually five, toured their part of town with the maypole, and it was set down at street corners. The girl who supported the maypole sat on a small stool. The others, dressed with special clothes made of paper, in pastel shades, had small crowns on their heads. They danced to a traditional song, "Round and round the maypole, merrily we go; ippy, chippy, churry, singing as we go!" The chorus was: "Hurrah, hurrah, hurrah May queen." They had a collecting box, of course.

Their brothers had a dodge for making money: they performed The Bear Dance. The lad who elected to be the bear wore an old sack over his head. There were holes to enable him to see. The bear's face was indicated by chalk marks; the ears were the stretched corners of the sack, tied with string. To the bear was attached a few yards of string. The lads stopped at street corners and the lad holding the string put the bear through its paces. The bear ran in a circle, and the traditional song was: "Arry om, pompay; arry om pompay; arry, array om pompay", with the first part at speed and the latter somewhat slower. Recalls the Burnley man: "Every now and again, the boss shouted out: 'Catch-a-poley', and he threw a broom handle to the bear, who caught it and tossed it back. A variation was when he said 'Over', when the bear did a forward somersault at the end of the string. After the performance, the collecting box was taken round."

Genuine bears appeared in the streets in Edwardian days. "The one I remember most clearly was an enormous creature, with as much white on its coat as brown. It couldn't have been a cross between a brown and a polar bear, but we children used to think it was. The thing was six feet high," I was told in Burnley. "The bear had a muzzle and was kept on the end of a chain, which was attached to a collar round its neck. This bear shuffled from one foot to the other, waving its forelegs about, and more or less covered a circle. Then, the collecting tin was produced. One day, when the performance was over, the man and his bear went to a piece of spare ground. I followed and I saw the man and bear sitting side by side. That bear had the same posture as the man—upright, with feet extended. The owner had produced a packet of food. He and the bear took a mouthful in turn. It was not wearing its muzzle, and the two sat together, just like old pals!"

Another man, of vaguely East European origin, appeared with a small, hand-operated organ on a stick. "Attached to this organ was a long stretch of rope. The other end was fastened to the collar on a monkey, which wore a jacket and a red fez cap. I watched a woman appear at an upstairs window. That monkey went up a fallpipe and crossed to the window holding out its hand for a coin, which it placed in the owner's tin!"

On summer days, before the 1914-18 war, German bands appeared. It was said that the bandsmen were spies! They wore splendid uniforms with peaked caps, and "they played the usual German stuff, mostly waltzes but with a few marches. Then someone went round with a tin." Street hawkers included Rag Jack, who stored his rags on a cart drawn by a donkey that was "starved to death, and didn't seem much bigger than a Labrador dog." His cart was literally tied up with string. Rag Jack would perch on the cart, and as they went round the back streets he called, melodically, lingeringly: "Any rags or bones today?" All the mothers who had naughty children would say to them: "Behave yourselves. Rag Jack's coming! He's shouting: 'Any boys or girls today?'"

Another street trader made a living out of clothes props, nothing else. He walked down every back street in town. As he passed a door, he kicked it with his clog. Clonk! Simultaneously he shouted: "Props!" Five seconds later, the next door was reached, and one heard another loud clonk, followed by a shouted "Props!"

The muffin man announced his presence with a bell. On his head was an enormous basket, lined with spotless linen. An equally clean piece of cloth covered his oatcakes—"proper oatcakes"—and crumpets and muffins. Oatcake might be spread with butter, then rolled up into sausage form, or hung over a creel, like washing. Next morning it was no longer soft, but dry and crisp.

The Lancashire street had a gala atmosphere every sunny evening. Children played. Parents gossiped or, sitting on the doorsteps, silently contemplated the world. Morris dancing was enjoyed, the dancers being accompanied by concertina bands. Brass bands and the chapel choirs toured the streets at Christmas.

On New Year's Eve, scores of men left their homes just before midnight, and their wives locked the doors behind them. The men loitered in the street until the church clock struck, and then they re-entered the houses to "let in the New Year". An Accrington man visited a friend one New Year's Eve and had to wait outside until nearly one o'clock on New Year's morning because a man with a black head of hair had not arrived to "let in" the New Year.

Few people stirred in the streets on winter evenings. A trader remembered clearly by a Nelson man was the hot-pea man who arrived swinging a bell and inviting custom for his mushy peas. The pie and pea man made his rounds with a little handcart. A brazier kept the food warm. The hot pie vendor had his wares wrapped in cotton cloths, held in a large basket, which he balanced on his head. "My brother and I could either have a cream horn from the confectioner or a hot pie. We had a bath on Friday night and—clean and tidy—we sat up in bed with mounting excitement, waiting for the pie man. Father stood at the door and invited him to enter the house. The pies he bought were then brought up to the bedroom. We ate them while sitting up in bed!"

Holiday Week

A DARWEN woman recalled: "One week's holiday—no pay. Christmas Day, Boxing Day and two days at September—all without pay. Good Friday, but not Easter Monday—broken pay." For 51 weeks the Lancashire mill town family thought of one week—the annual Fair or Wakes. A Burnley man told me: "Be reights, it was Fair Week." And what a fair was held in the cattle market. "You couldn't count the roundabouts. There were scores of hawkers and catchpennies. I remember a chap with a little cage propped on a stand. There were two love birds in the cage. Alongside it was a little trough holding a lot of tickets, like bus tickets but a little thicker. If you gave one of the love birds a penny, it took the money off you, dropped it in a box, then picked up one of these cards and gave it you. On that card was your 'fortune'."

He continued, with zest: "If you had a penny, you could buy a bag of brandy snaps half as big as your head. Then there were toys. I've bought a trumpet for a penny. That trumpet was wrapped up in silver thread and had tassels on it, also a little flag. You could play three or four notes on it."

Every kind of gambling was practised at the annual fair. Wrestling booths were luridly decorated. A small-scale circus vied for popularity. "There were fishing stalls where you chucked a line with a magnet over the top and picked up a little number: you got a present according to the number. That was just the start of the fair week. Everybody was there. There was an awful row!"

In Wakes Week, people had their annual reminder of how dirty was the normal atmosphere in town. "Except for that week, nobody really understood what clear skies were like. Then every factory was shut down; the shops were closed. At Burnley, if you hadn't got a week's supply of bread, you'd to walk either to Brierfield in one direction, or over to Padiham in another."

When the skies cleared, people went to the summit of Pendle Hill, or to a vantage point like Crown Point at Burnley, to look around: to ponder on Pennine highspots like Penyghent and Ingleborough, which would not be seen again for twelve months. It was said at Bolton that Wakes Week was the only time you could see the Welsh hills from the back of the town. It so happened that Leigh and Wigan were on holiday at the same time.

Pendle Hill was the attraction for thousands. "On Good Friday, we climbed Pendle Hill from Colne," said a local woman. "Each of us had a carrier bag with some butties and a bottle of water or milk; it depended on what we could afford. We went in clogs because they were warm. We were all singing as we walked through Barrowford to Barley, then on to the Big End of Pendle." A Burnley man told me of going through Newchurch to Barley, and afterwards walking on to Roughlee for a jug of tea in the old mill and a walk by the lake.

Such modest pleasures were for those who were not intending to go away for a holiday. Most people contrived to leave town. Blackpool was Mecca to them; others enjoyed quieter pleasures at Morecambe and St. Annes. Some embarked on steamers sailing from Fleetwood to the Isle of Man. The stay-at-homes inhabited an almost empty town. Their friends "blew in" a year's savings by the sea.

A Bolton man told me: "Everybody was in what was called a Diddle 'em Club. They put in so much a week and drew out the money just before Wakes Week. Every year, or so it seemed, someone ran off with the money belonging to one of the clubs. There would be a hue and cry for it. In the 1930s you needed only £4 or £5 to take a family on a week's holiday. For your digs, you'd pay about £2 for the week. If you were really posh you could have a private sitting room."

The railways were congested as Wakes Week began. At Bolton,

where it was necessary to go down some steps, people despaired of getting themselves and their luggage on the same train. The railways had arrangements to issue tickets in advance, and for 2s. would collect luggage and ensure its delivery. Yet half mile long queues formed at the stations. A man who worked "railway specials" from Hellifield into Blackpool in the days of the L & Y arrived in Clitheroe to see so many people on the platforms they were being controlled by railway police. "When I stopped the train, there was a mad scramble to get on." As a youngster, heading for a Blackpool holiday, he once counted 24 people in a single compartment. The guard's brake was always full. Up to the early 1930s, there might be 3,000 people leaving Clitheroe alone. "When you stopped at Blackpool, and looked down the platform, all you saw was a sea of familiar faces."

A memory of Barracks Station, Burnley, as it was before the 1914-18 war, is of porters with sleeved waistcoats standing at the edge of the platform, urging the mass of people to stand back as a train arrived. "When the train came in, every window was packed with passengers, looking out. Kids were hanging out, clutching their buckets and spades and bunches of flags. You had to fight to get a seat."

The holiday was felt to have begun as the train left Preston. "All the children looked out of the window until one of them saw the Tower at Blackpool. Then there was a mighty cheer. Someone reported seeing the Big Wheel. A real shout went up—the sound carried all down the train."

Blackpool, Southport and Morecambe were the main holiday resorts for the cotton towns. Blackpool was far and away the most popular. It was created as a show centre with the Lancashire families mainly in mind. In 1919, some 10,000 people from Nelson alone stayed at Blackpool for at least four days. That same week, 1,000 people were at Southport and 500 made the crossing to the Isle of Man. The Blackpool landladies watched the hosts staggering to their front doors. The visitors had the familiar sight of a dining room window in which was set a table with the obligatory three bottles—brown sauce, tomato ketchup, vinegar.

It was customary for a family to take to Blackpool as much of their own food as they could manage to handle. Prepared well in advance, it was augmented by fresh food purchased at the resort. The family baking travelled in a tin trunk. Even the week's supply of meat might be taken. The landlady would ask: "Are ter goin' to board?" or "Do I do t'lot for thee?" Most families, very cost-conscious, merely took rooms and the landlady cooked their food for them. A Burnley man says: "Everything was costed to the last penny. If you went to a show on the pier, and was charged twopence for something instead of the expected penny, then your holiday plans were thrown askew. You would be hard up by week-end!" Self-catering continued to a lessening degree until the 1930s.

Mill lasses, who had been saving for 51 weeks so that they could have a beano at Blackpool on the 52nd week, were determined to enjoy themselves. Some, with extravagance, hired a horse cab at Talbot Road station at Blackpool and were conveyed to Yates's Wine Lodge, where port and lemon were ordered. A Bolton man remembers their determination to meet a boy. "Sometimes it led to better things; sometimes to worse things. If a group of girls went to a boarding house, it was likely there was a group of boys at the same digs. Each mill girl would talk for weeks afterwards about the boy she met at Blackpool." The evenings were spent dancing at the Tower Ballroom. "There was a very good dance band called Bertini's, and Reginald Dixon presided at the theatre organ. The theme song of the Lancashire holidaymakers was: 'I do like to be beside the Seaside'."

How a Colne family, though poverty-stricken, spent a week at Blackpool was told to me by one of the family. "Grandfather—who was a blacksmith—won some money at his local pub; we called it *The Rat Pit,* because it stood near some waste ground by the river. He said to mother: 'You need a holiday; I'll pay for travel and board. Take grannie'. It was Wakes Week. The train took about four hours to get to Blackpool. When it went into a siding, everybody leaned out of the window, waving at everybody else. We stayed in Yorkshire Street, which was well-known for the number of people it could sleep. Grannie, mother, my sister and me had a double bedroom. My brother went into a room with the lads of another family.

"Mother catered for herself; the landlady cooked the food. I remember that when we were getting ready for that holiday, she bought some new black stockings, put eggs in paper, slipped the eggs into a stocking, one at a time, tying bits of string between them, and not one was cracked when we reached Blackpool. Each family had a shelf in a cupboard on which to put their food. Grannie was on her best behaviour. She usually smoked a pipe. That holiday, we'd see her sitting on the bed — smoking a cigarette!"

A Nelson man, taken as a child to Blackpool, linked the place with some of his most impressive experiences. "I remember getting off the holiday special at Central Station. The distance between Blackpool Tower and home in the mind of a child was infinity. Home was miles away, over there ... We'd finished with it for a week. There was a sort of freedom about the place. And even in my time—the early 1930s—mother went to the Blackpool shops every morning to buy the food we needed. She gave the food to the landlady, who cooked it. We might appear to be affluent as we walked down the prom., but we couldn't afford full board."

The return home had its own ceremonial. A child was despatched to a neighbour's home to collect the household pets. Presents were distributed. A popular gift was a plate with a series of holes near the edge through which a ribbon was threaded. Comedians bought an item such as a small pot lavatory or a tea cup that was, in effect, only half a cup; it had been sliced vertically down the middle, with the inscription: "You asked for half a cup of tea; now you've got it." Every relative had to have a "bit o' summat", and most of them received lettered rock. "You had been to Blackpool, and had been a millionaire. You'd lived like a lord. That had come to an end. On the first Monday back, likely as not, you dined on bread and jam," said a friend whose childhood was spent in Burnley.

Outings to the seaside were possible in other than Wakes Week. Benevolent mill-owners treated their workers before the 1914-18 war. At Belmont, near Bolton, the management paid all expenses for a works trip to Blackpool in 1893, and the workforce was away from home for nearly 17 hours. The firm also arranged a trip to Wembley for the Imperial Exhibition.

A number of enterprising families managed to acquire a second home in the country by having an old bus body tucked away somewhere. A field at Overhouses Farm, at the bottom of Pendle, was covered by little huts and old buses.

Time for Leisure

D EMON Drink reared his sozzled head in the Lancashire towns. Yet in 1903, when the spirit of reform began to affect the licensing laws, black lists of habitual drunkards were being circulated to publicans at Bolton. No one with a name on the list should receive more than one drink. The public house was the man's world to which a woman was grudgingly admitted at weekends, if at all.

The centre of town seethed with activity on Saturday evenings, especially in the period before the 1914-18 war. At Burnley, three theatres provided live entertainment. The largest, known as the *Palace,* had a "flasher" on its façade. "We used to stand outside watching the bright colours—white, red, green—flashing across the face of the sign," it is recalled. "The impression of great prosperity lasted until it was seen that the lads selling copies of the 'pink', the special Saturday sporting edition of the *Northern Daily Telegraph*, were with bare feet. They were grubby beyond words." A man sold shoe laces, cadging a penny or two that would provide him with admission to a common lodging house. Among the match-sellers was one with a husky voice. His halfpenny box of matches was a pretext for begging. Most people— relaxed by the Saturday evening air of contentment—would give him a penny or tuppence. I heard it said that when the man died he left over £20,000. A music hall song popular at that time related to mashers, an expression meaning dandies. The song was called *The Two Burnley Mashers.*

The cinema was to have a considerable effect on working class attitudes towards life and art forms. It was in being on a regular commercial basis before the 1914-18 war. Two films recalled at Burnley were *Black Beauty* and *The Fall of Troy,* the latter being the classical story of the wooden horse. It was, in effect, a colour film—colour in the sense that the sequence showing Troy on fire had been printed on film that was tinted red! Early audiences at the "flicks" were sober and appreciative. Later, during the so-called "flea pit" days, there might be such an uproar that the manager had to stop the film and remonstrate with the most noisy patrons.

Cricket, the main outdoor attraction in summer, drew thousands to the county matches. "Even the Lancashire League was high-powered stuff that received support from the masses," I heard at Nelson, where Leary Constantine was a professional. One visiting cricketer who bowled out Leary was told by an angry supporter: "We've come to see Leary bat, not you bowl!" The crowd participated. One man, good at quips, shouted to a bowler: "Tha's getten t'batsman in two minds. He doesn't know whether to clout thee for four or six!"

Snooker and billiards, crown green bowling and tennis were other popular sports, but—recalls the Nelson man—"if you played tennis in the old days, you were considered to be something of a sissy."

Every town had its organised group of naturalists. The Bacup Natural History Society was founded in 1878, the first lecture being given by Mr. Henry Kerr, who had visited the sea birds on Walney Island, off Barrow-in-Furness. In spring and summer, outings were organised. In winter, members of the societies sat in semi-darkness, with the warm glow from multi-tinted slides on their faces, as the most intrepid members told of their experiences in far distant places.